NOAH'S
KNITS

NOAH'S
KNITS

FIONA GOBLE

**Andrews McMeel
Publishing, LLC**

Kansas City • Sydney • London

Noah's Knits

Andrews McMeel Publishing, LLC
an Andrews McMeel Universal company
1130 Walnut Street, Kansas City, Missouri 64106
www.andrewsmcmeel.com

ISBN: 978-1-4494-0979-1

Library of Congress Control Number: 2011932635

This book was conceived, designed, and produced by
Ivy Press
210 High Street, Lewes
East Sussex BN7 2NS, UK
www.ivy-group.co.uk

Creative Director *Peter Bridgewater*
Publisher *Jason Hook*
Editorial Director *Tom Kitch*
Senior Designer *James Lawrence*
Designer *Clare Barber*
Story text *Gill Paul*
Photographer *Andrew Perris*
Illustrator *Ivan Hissey*

Printed in China

Color origination by Ivy Press Reprographics

12 13 14 15 16 IYP 10 9 8 7 6 5 4 3 2 1

IMPORTANT!
Safety warning: Many of the knitted figures are small or have removable parts, making them a choking hazard. They are not suitable for children under the age of three.

ATTENTION: SCHOOLS AND BUSINESSES
Andrews McMeel books are available at quantity discounts with bulk purchase for educational, business, or sales promotional use. For information, please e-mail the Andrews McMeel Publishing Special Sales Department: specialsales@amuniversal.com

Contents

Introduction

Two of parenthood's great pleasures are reading stories to and playing with your child or children. This book brings these pleasures together with the story of Noah and his Ark and patterns for knitting Noah, Mrs. Noah, and the animals. Even though the knitted figures are full of character, they're straightforward to make if you can knit, purl, increase, and decrease.

Part of the joy of knitting your own toys is that it's both very relaxing and also thoroughly rewarding to see how the projects come together. But creating the dolls is only the beginning of the fun—soon you'll have enough pairs of animals to let you and your child read the story together while playing with your knitted creations. As the number of occupants of the Ark increases, you can enjoy reading the story all over again (and perhaps your child can add the appropriate sound effects as each animal comes onboard). There is even a cardboard Ark in the back of the book for your child to play with.

CREATING YOUR MENAGERIE

The projects in this book vary in complexity, so even if you're new to knitting, you'll soon be able to create a pair of cute little monkeys or bouncing bunny rabbits. Once you're comfortable with creating the smaller projects, you'll be able to move on to slightly more complex animals, such as the goats and bears, before finally tackling the elephants and giraffes. You don't need to make all of the animals right away; instead, you can make them in quiet moments over several months or even longer, building up the population of the Ark as you go along. And the knitting doesn't have to end once you've created all of the projects in this book—you can continue creating new creatures, using the patterns in this book and your imagination as your inspirations.

A Pair of Needles and a Ball of Yarn

To knit Noah and his motley crew, just about all you need are a pair of knitting needles and a ball of yarn. If you're a knitting enthusiast already, you probably have everything you need to get going right away. But just in case, here's a list of essentials. You will find them all in your local craft or yarn store.

KNITTING NEEDLES

The main parts of all the projects are knitted using size 2/3 (3 mm) knitting needles. You will also need pairs of size 1 (2.25 mm) and size 2 (2.75 mm) needles to knit some of the smaller parts, such as some of the beaks, ears, and tails. As the projects are small, it makes sense to choose shorter needles. If you have a choice, opt for the needles with the most pointed ends, because this makes it easier to get between the stitches on tightly knitted pieces.

A CROCHET HOOK

There is no real crochet involved in the projects, but you do need to know how to make simple crochet chains for some of the animals' manes and tails. We recommend that you use a size D-3 (3.25 mm) crochet hook, but a hook that is slightly larger or smaller will work just as well.

A YARN OR TAPESTRY NEEDLE

You will need a large-eye needle with a relatively blunt end to sew the pieces of your project together.

AN EMBROIDERY NEEDLE

You will need an embroidery needle to embroider the eyes and some of the other features of the dolls. Embroidery needles are sharper than yarn and tapestry needles. Choose a needle with a large eye, so that you can thread your yarn through it more easily.

A STANDARD SEWING NEEDLE

You will need an ordinary sewing needle to sew the button onto Noah's belt.

SAFETY PINS

For some of the projects, you will need a few small safety pins to hold some of your knitting stitches while you work on a different section of your knitting.

A STITCH HOLDER

You will need a stitch holder or large safety pin to hold some of your knitting stitches while you work on a different section of your knitting.

A WATER-SOLUBLE PEN

This pen is very useful for marking the position of the features and markings on the creatures before you embroider them. Water-soluble pens look and work like ordinary felt-tip pens, but the ink disappears when you spray or dab it with water. They are available at most craft stores.

A RED CRAYON

The rosy look on Noah's and Mrs. Noah's cheeks is made using an ordinary red crayon.

A PAIR OF SMALL SCISSORS

You will need a pair of small, sharp scissors to trim the yarn tails after you have finished embroidering the dolls' and animals' features.

A TAPE MEASURE OR RULER

You will need a tape measure or a ruler to check the length of some of your pieces.

YARN

Almost all the projects are knitted using standard double knitting (DK) yarn. The exact requirements for each project are given on the relevant pages.

It does not matter if you mix brands of yarn within a particular project. You will not necessarily get better results from using the most expensive yarns, but we highly recommend that you use yarns that are either 100 percent wool or have a high wool content—for example, yarns that are 50 percent wool and 50 percent acrylic. Yarns that are 100 percent acrylic or 100 percent cotton are not recommended because they are too dense and lack the elasticity of wool and wool-based yarns.

For a few of the projects, you will also need some mohair yarn or a yarn spun from a blend of mohair and silk. Mohair yarn is very light and fluffy and is made from the coat of Angora goats.

Each of the projects in this book includes estimates for the length and weight of the yarns you will need to complete the project. Because the exact quantity you will use will depend to some extent on the type and brand of yarn you choose and the tension of your knitting, please use the numbers as only a guideline.

POLYESTER TOY FILLING

The toys are stuffed with 100 percent polyester toy filling. This is a soft, fluffy material specially manufactured for stuffing toys and other handmade objects. You can buy it in sewing and craft stores. Always make sure that the filling you buy conforms to all relevant safety standards.

ORDINARY SEWING THREAD

For one of the projects, you will need a small amount of standard sewing thread to sew on a button.

ABBREVIATIONS AND GAUGE

*/**	these mark the start and end of a section of the knitting pattern to be repeated later when instructed		the slipped stitch over the stitch just knitted)	in.	inch(es)
		pwise	by purling the stitch(es)	mm	millimeter(s)
( )	repeat the directions within the parentheses the number of times indicated before continuing	rem	remaining	m	meter(s)
		rep	repeat	oz.	ounce(s)
		rs	right side	yd.	yard(s)
beg	beginning	s1	slip one (slip a stitch onto the right-hand needle without knitting it)		
cont	continue				
inc1	increase one stitch (by knitting into the same stitch twice)			**GAUGE**	
		ssk	slip, slip, knit (slip 2 stitches one at a time knitwise, then knit the 2 slipped stitches together)	The general knitting gauge for the patterns in this book is 12 sts and 16 rows to 1½ in. (4 cm) square over St st on 2 or 3 (3 mm) needles.	
incl	including				
K	knit				
k2tog	knit the next 2 stitches together	ssp	slip, slip, purl (slip 2 stitches one at a time purlwise, then purl the 2 slipped stitches together	When you are knitting small items, gauge is not as important as when you are making clothes. However, it is important that the knitted fabric you produce is fairly tight or your projects may look misshapen and the stuffing will show through. If your tension is significantly looser, you should choose needles a size smaller than those suggested. If your tension is significantly tighter, choose needles a size larger.	
kwise	by knitting the stitch(es)				
m1	make one stitch (by picking up the horizontal loop lying before the next stitch and knitting into the back of it)	st(s)	stitch(es)		
		St st	stockinette stitch		
		ws	wrong side		
P	purl				
p2tog	purl the next 2 stitches together	cm	centimeter(s)		
psso	pass slipped stitch over (pass	g	gram(s)		

Knit One, Purl One

If you want to brush up your knitting skills, check the information below to find out how to start and stop your work, how to knit and purl, and how to shape your work into the pieces you need to create Noah, his charming wife, and his menagerie.

CASTING ON

This method of casting on is known as the cable method and requires two knitting needles.

1 Create a slipknot by making a loop in the yarn and pulling another loop of yarn through it. Transfer this loop onto the needle. Tighten it by pulling on the yarn "tail." This slipknot forms your first cast-on stitch. Hold this needle in your left hand (if you are right-handed).

2 Put the tip of your right-hand needle through the front of the first cast-on stitch and under the left-hand needle. Now wind the yarn around the tip of the right-hand needle.

3 Using your needle tip, draw the yarn through the first cast-on stitch to form a loop.

4 Place the loop on your left-hand needle to form the second stitch.

5 To make the third stitch, insert the tip of your right-hand needle between the two cast-on stitches. Wind the yarn around the needle from left to right, as before.

6 Draw your yarn through the gap between the stitches as before to form another loop. Then transfer the loop to your left-hand needle.

Repeat the last two steps until you have cast on the required number of stitches.

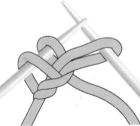

KNITTING STITCHES

There are two basic knitting stitches—the knit stitch and the purl stitch. All other stitches are a combination or slight variation of these two stitches. If you knit every row, your knitted fabric is called garter stitch. If you work alternate rows of knit and purl stitches, your knitted fabric is called stockinette stitch. This is the most widely used combination of stitches and is the main combination used for the patterns here. If you work a combination of knit and purl stitches in each row, you can produce a variety of patterns, including the seed stitch used for the upper bodies of the crocodiles.

THE KNIT STITCH

1 Holding the needle with the cast-on stitches in your left hand, insert the tip of your right-hand needle into the front of the first cast-on stitch, from left to right.

2 Wind the yarn around the tip of the right-hand needle, from left to right.

3 Using the tip of the right-hand needle, pull the yarn through the stitch to form a loop. This loop is the new stitch.

4 Slip the original stitch off the left-hand needle by pulling the right-hand needle to the right.

THE PURL STITCH

1 Holding the needle with the stitches in your left hand, insert the tip of the right-hand needle into the front of the first stitch, from right to left.

2 Wind the yarn around the tip of the right-hand needle from right to left.

3 Using the tip of the right-hand needle, pull the yarn through the stitch to form a loop. This loop is the new stitch.

4 Slip the original stitch off the left-hand needle by pulling the right-hand needle to the right.

BINDING OFF

Binding off links the stitches together so that they will not unravel.

BINDING OFF KNITWISE

For most of the projects you will need to bind off knitwise, which means that you knit the stitches before binding them off.

1 Knit two stitches in the normal way. Using the tip of the left-hand needle, lift the first stitch you have just knitted over the second.

2 You now have just one stitch on the right-hand needle; you can see that there is a neat loop across the top of the first cast-off stitch, so the yarn cannot unravel.

Knit another stitch, so you have two stitches on your right-hand needle once more, and lift the first stitch over the second. Repeat this process until you have just one stitch left. Trim the yarn, leaving a tail long enough to sew your work together. Pull the yarn tail all the way through the last stitch to secure your work.

BINDING OFF PURLWISE

In a few of the projects, you will need to bind off purlwise. This is just like binding off knitwise, except that you purl the stitches rather than knit them.

1 Purl two stitches in the normal way. Using the tip of the left-hand needle, lift the first stitch you have just purled over the second.

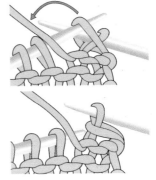

2 As in casting off knitwise, you now have just one stitch on the right-hand needle.

Purl another stitch, so that you have two stitches on your right-hand needle once more, and lift the first stitch over the second. Repeat this process until you have just one stitch left. Trim the yarn, leaving a tail long enough to sew your work together. Pull the yarn tail all the way through the last stitch to secure your work.

CHANGING COLOR

For some of the projects—for example, the zebras and the goats—you need to know how to change from one yarn color to another on the same piece while you are knitting. This process is very straightforward.

If you have finished with the yarn you have just knitted and don't need it again or don't need it for several rows, simply break that yarn and join the new color. Once you have knitted a few stitches in the new color, you can pull the two yarn tails a little to make sure your knitting is firm and tie them together in a simple knot.

If you are going to use the yarn you have just finished with again in a few rows' time, leave it by the side of your work but don't break it. Simply join in the new yarn and start knitting with it. You may find it is a little loose at the beginning, but you can see to it once you have finished. When you need the original color again, just take it up the side of your work, remembering not to pull it tightly.

In, Out, and Around About

To shape the pieces needed for the dolls and animals in this book, you need to know how to increase and decrease the number of stitches on your needles.

INCREASING

Two methods of increasing are used in the patterns in this book. The method that you use depends on where the extra stitch is needed.

INCREASING BY MAKING AN ADDITIONAL STITCH (M1)

1 With the tip of your right-hand needle, pick up the horizontal strand that runs between the stitch you have just knitted and the next stitch.

2 Transfer the strand to your left-hand needle by inserting the needle through the front of the strand from right to left.

3 Knit through the back of the picked-up strand to form a new stitch.

Occasionally, you will need to make an additional stitch purlwise.

INCREASING BY KNITTING TWICE INTO THE SAME STITCH (INC1)

Knit the stitch in the normal way, but do not slip the original stitch off the needle. Instead, knit into the back of it, then slide it off the needle. The instruction "inc1" in the pattern means that you make an additional stitch when knitting the next stitch.

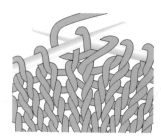

DECREASING

You need to know a few techniques for decreasing the number of stitches on your needle, depending on where you are making the decrease and how many stitches you need to decrease.

KNIT TWO STITCHES TOGETHER (K2TOG)

This is just like knitting a single stitch, but you put your needle from left to right through the front of two stitches instead of one. Then simply knit the stitch in the normal way.

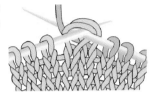

PURL TWO STITCHES (P2TOG)

This is just like purling a single stitch, but you put your needle from right to left through the front of two stitches instead of one. Then simply purl the stitch in the normal way.

SLIP TWO STITCHES, THEN KNIT THEM TOGETHER (SSK)

Slip one stitch and then the next from your left- to your right-hand needle, without knitting them. Then insert your left-hand needle through the front of both these stitches and knit them together.

SLIP TWO STITCHES, THEN PURL THEM TOGETHER (SSP)

This technique is like ssk (above), but you purl the stitches instead of knitting them. It is used only occasionally in these patterns. Slip one stitch and then the next from your left- to your right-hand needle, without purling them. Then insert your left-hand needle through the front of both these stitches and purl them together.

SLIP A STITCH, KNIT A STITCH, AND PASS THE SLIPPED STITCH OVER (S1, K1, PSSO)

This technique is similar to the ssk method of decreasing, but it produces a slightly different look, which makes it more suitable in some situations. First slip a stitch from your left- to your right-hand needle, without knitting it, then knit the next stitch. Then lift the slipped stitch over the stitch you have just knitted.

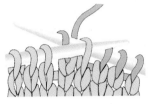

SLIP A STITCH, KNIT TWO STITCHES TOGETHER, AND PASS THE SLIPPED STITCH OVER (S1, K2TOG, PSSO)

This method of decreasing reduces the number of stitches by two and is a combination of some of the techniques described above.

1 First, slip a stitch from your left- to your right-hand needle, without knitting it. Then knit the next two stitches together.

2 Using the tip of your left-hand needle, lift the slipped stitch over the stitch in front.

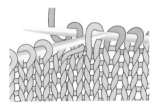

Occasionally, you will need to work this decrease purlwise.

Let's Get It All Together

Once you've finished knitting all the pieces for your character or animal, it's time to sew them together. This is easy to do, but it is worth taking your time with it, particularly if you are new to knitting small items such as these. These pages describe the different techniques you will need.

MATTRESS STITCH

You can use this stitch to join two straight vertical edges (the sides of your rows), two horizontal edges (cast-on or bound-off edges), or one vertical and one horizontal edge. Mattress stitch is worked on the right side of your work. Once completed, it is virtually invisible, particularly when joining vertical edges.

VERTICAL EDGES

Place the two vertical edges together. Take the yarn under the running stitch between the first two stitches on one side, and then under the running stitch between the first two stitches on the other side. Continue doing this, pulling the yarn up fairly tight every few stitches.

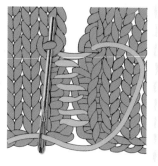

HORIZONTAL EDGES

Place the two horizontal edges together. Take the yarn under the two "legs" on one edge, and then under the two "legs" on the corresponding edge. Continue doing this, pulling the yarn up fairly tightly every few stitches.

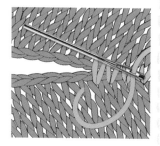

WHIPSTITCHING

It is not practical to use mattress stitch to join the seams on small items or on items with curved edges. In this kind of situation, you will need to whipstitch them instead. Whipstitching is normally worked with the right sides of the two pieces you are joining facing each other.

To work the stitch, bring the needle out on the front of your work a little way in from the edge. Then take the needle over the edge of the seam and bring it back out at the front again. Continue in this way until the seam is complete.

RUNNING STITCH

Simply insert your needle into your fabric a stitch's width along, then back out again a little farther on. Repeat this process until you have completed the seam, making sure your stitches are evenly spaced and firm. You can usually work a few running stitches at a time.

PICK UP AND KNIT

Occasionally, you will need to pick up and knit some stitches along a bound-off edge. With the right side of your work facing you, insert the right-hand needle between the running threads of the first two stitches, then knit the stitch in the normal way.

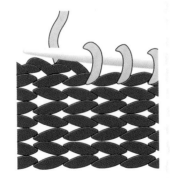

STUFFING

It is important not to overstuff your characters and animals, or they will look lumpy and out of shape. Use a little stuffing at a time, pulling it between your fingers to fluff it up a little before you use it.

JOINING SMALL PIECES TO LARGER ONES

The neatest way to join the animals' legs to their bodies is to use a version of mattress stitch. Take your yarn under a couple of yarn threads on the leg and then under a couple of yarn threads on the body, pulling your yarn up tightly every few stitches.

Alternatively, you can whipstitch the legs in place. Whipstitching is also the easiest way to sew on the animals' ears and tails.

THE FINAL FINISH

When you have stitched your items together, you will have some loose yarn tails that need hiding. On the main body of the animals, simply thread the yarn tail back into the body and out at another point. You may need to run the yarn tail down the side of a small body part such as an ear before you do this. Then, squeeze the body slightly and trim the yarn tail closely. When the body springs back into shape, the yarn tail will disappear inside.

You will need to conceal the yarn tails on some of Noah's and Mrs. Noah's clothes by working a few running stitches forward and then backward in the seam.

Sometimes when you have stitched an item together, the flat pieces look slightly curled or your item is simply not exactly the shape you want. If this happens, soak the item in cold water. Squeeze out the excess water, reshape the item, and let it dry.

A Touch of Crochet and Embroidery

Facial features and hair are what will give Noah, Mrs. Noah, and all of their animals their individual characteristics, so you need to know how to create a simple crochet chain and how to work a few basic embroidery stitches.

HOW TO CROCHET A CHAIN

A simple crochet chain is used to make some of the animals' tails and manes.

1 Make a slipknot on your crochet hook in the same way as when beginning to cast on some knitting. Holding the slipknot in place, wind the yarn around the hook from the back to the front and catch the yarn in the crochet hook tip.

2 Pull the yarn through the loop on your hook to make the second stitch of your crochet chain.

Continue like this until your chain is the length you want it to be.

ADDING EMBROIDERED FEATURES

To add the features to your dolls and animals, you need to know a few basic embroidery stitches, which are worked in yarn or split lengths of yarn.

STARTING AND FINISHING YOUR STITCHES

To begin, tie a simple knot or double knot at the end of your yarn. Insert the needle from the back of your work in an inconspicuous area between stitches. Bring it out on the front of the work at the point where you want to start stitching. Pull the yarn firmly, so that the knot slips between the stitches and is hidden somewhere in the stuffing.

When you have finished, bring the needle out at an inconspicuous area of your work. Pull the yarn gently, making sure that your work stays in shape. Secure the yarn

by working a couple of small stitches, one over the other, in the running stitches between the knitted stitches (these will be slightly sunken). Then conceal the yarn tail (see page 15).

When working embroidery stitches, always take the needle between the strands that make up the yarn instead of between the knitting stitches. This technique will help make your embroidery secure and ensure that your knitting stitches do not become distorted.

STRAIGHT STITCH

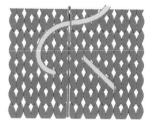

Bring the needle out on the front of your work at the point where you want the stitch the start, then insert it back into your work at the point where you want the stitch to end. To make some of the mouths, you will need to make two or three straight stitches in a V or Y shape.

SATIN STITCH

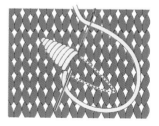

This stitch is really a row of straight stitches worked closely together. Bring your needle out at your starting point. Insert the needle back into your work to the right and out again, just below your starting point. Continue in this way until the shape is filled. Be careful to avoid pulling your yarn too tightly or your work will pucker.

FRENCH KNOTS

Bring the needle out at the point where you want to work the stitch. With the needle close to the surface of the knitting, wind the yarn twice around the needle (or once if you want the pupils to be a little smaller). Then insert the tip of your needle back into your work, just next to the starting point, and pull it all the way through; you may find it helpful to hold the wrapped yarn in place with your thumbnail as you do so.

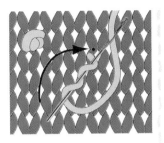

CHAIN STITCH

Bring the needle out at your starting point. Insert the needle back into your work just to the side of your starting point, and bring it out again a stitch's length away, making sure that the needle tip lies over the loop you have just formed. Pull the yarn up tightly so that the stitch looks fairly tight and firm.

Making the Ark

At the back of this book, you'll find a cardboard Ark. Constructing the Ark will be a lot simpler for you than it was for Noah—all you will need is a straightedge, a butter knife or other blunt tool for scoring folds, a pair of scissors, a craft knife, and some white glue.

1 First, cut out the hull, superstructure, gangplank, and gangplank support using a pair of scissors.

2 To make the Ark, cut out the two windows using a craft knife (work slowly and carefully to make sure you have a neat hole), then cut along the center and top of the double doors. Next, use a straightedge and a butter knife to score along the edges of the doors and along the supports at the bow and stern of the boat.

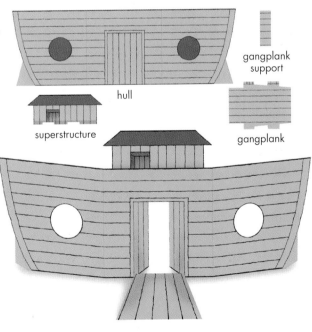

gangplank support

hull

superstructure

gangplank

3 Apply a little white glue (PVA adhesive) to the bottom of the front of the superstructure, then glue it to the top of the hull.

4 To make the gangplank, use a straightedge and a butter knife to score along the blue lines. Fold the end of the gangplank and glue it to the tabs on the base with the white glue. Glue the gangplank support to the other two tabs. You now have your finished Ark, complete with opening doors and a gangplank. Use the supports at the bow and stern of the Ark to help support it.

God Tells Noah to Build the Ark

When God first created the world and all the plants, animals, and people in it, everything was perfect, and He was very pleased with His work. The first man and woman, Adam and Eve, had children; then their children had children, who also had children; and as the world got bigger, the people living in it became more and more wicked. They lied and they stole, they fought and they killed each other, and that made God very sad. He began to regret that He had created human beings in the first place. At last, He could stand it no longer and He decided to destroy all the living creatures on the earth and start again.

However, there existed one genuinely good man, whose name was Noah. He was just and kind, and God could find no fault with him, so He decided that Noah and his family alone would be saved. He came to Noah to tell him of His plans.

"I will bring a flood of waters upon the earth, to destroy all flesh. Cattle and fowl, man and beast, and all creeping things . . . everything that is on the earth shall die," God told him.

Noah was understandably terrified when he heard this, but God went on to give him instructions that would help him to save his own family. He told him to make a huge Ark of gopher wood, lined inside and out with pitch. It should have three floors and a lot of separate rooms, with a large door set in the side and a roof. Trembling from head to foot, Noah promised God that he would do as He asked.

With the help of his three sons, Shem, Ham, and Japheth, Noah built the Ark just as God had ordered. They chopped down trees and sawed the wood into smooth planks, then nailed the planks together and coated them with pitch to make the Ark waterproof.

Noah

If you know you're going to have to face weeks of inclement weather, it pays to be properly prepared. So in addition to his work apron, Noah has his own heavy-duty raincoat and waterproof hat and a pair of green rubber boots. His jeans and sweater are knitted as part of the main figure. The apron, raincoat, hat, and boots are knitted separately.

You will need

FOR THE DOLL

¼ oz./8 g (20 yd./18 m) of beige DK yarn

⅛ oz./4 g (10 yd./9 m) of pale blue DK yarn

¼ oz./7 g (18 yd./16 m) of purple DK yarn

Small amounts of gray and dark brown DK yarn

Very small amounts of black, cream, and red DK yarn

¾ oz./20 g of polyester toy filling

A red crayon for coloring the cheeks

FOR THE CLOTHES

⅛ oz./4 g (10 yd./9 m) of orange DK yarn

¾ oz./22 g (58 yd./53 m) of bright yellow DK yarn

¼ oz./5 g (13 yd./12 m) of olive green DK yarn

A small green button for the raincoat buckle

Use size 2/3 (3 mm) knitting needles, except when instructed to use size 1 (2.25 mm) knitting needles, and a size D-3 (3.25 mm) crochet hook

DOLL

LEGS, BODY, AND HEAD

Noah's legs, body, and head are knitted as one piece, from the feet upward. The jeans and sweater are knitted as part of the doll.

Make 1

- Cast on 24 sts in beige for the first foot.
- Work 6 rows in St st, beg with a K row.
- Next row: K6, bind off 12 sts, K to end. [12 sts]
- Work 3 rows in St st, beg with a P row.
- Break yarn and join pale blue yarn.
- K 4 rows.
- Work 10 rows in St st, beg with a K row.
- Break yarn and leave sts on a spare needle or stitch holder.
- Knit the second foot and leg in exactly the same way but do not break yarn.
- Next row: K9 across second leg, put last 3 sts on a safety pin.
- On first leg, put first 3 sts on a safety pin, K6, put last 3 sts on a safety pin.
- Next row: P to last 3 sts, put these 3 sts on a safety pin.

Work on the 12 sts remaining on the needle.

- Work 4 rows in St st, beg with a K row.
- * Break yarn and join purple yarn.
- K 4 rows.
- Work 12 rows in St st, beg with a K row.
- Next row: Bind off 2 sts, K to end. [10 sts]
- Rep last row once. [8 sts]
- Break yarn.
- Rejoin beige yarn.
- Work 2 rows in St st, beg with a K row.
- Next row: (K1, m1) twice, K4, (m1, K1) twice. [12 sts]
- Next row: P.
- Next row: (K1, m1) 3 times, K6, (m1, K1) 3 times. [18 sts]
- Next row: P.
- Next row: K2, m1, K14, m1, K2. [20 sts] **

- Next row: P10, m1 pwise, P10. [21 sts]
- Next row: K10, K into front and back of made st, turn and P these 2 sts, turn again, and K to end. [22 sts]
- Next row: P9, p2tog, ssp, P9. [20 sts]
- Next row: K8, k2tog, ssk, K8. [18 sts]
- Next row: P.
- Next row: K2, (k2tog) 3 times, K2, (ssk) 3 times, K2. [12 sts]
- Next row: P1, (p2tog) twice, P2, (ssp) twice, P1. [8 sts]
- Next row: K1, k2tog, K2, ssk, K1. [6 sts]
- Bind off pwise.

- With pale blue yarn and with ws of work facing you, pick up and P 12 sts across back of legs.
- Work 6 rows in St st, beg with a K row.
- Work as for front side from * to **.
- Next row: P.
- Next row: K.
- Rep last 2 rows once.
- Next row: p2tog, P to last 2 sts, p2tog. [18 sts]
- Next row: K2, (k2tog) 3 times, K2, (ssk) 3 times, K2. [12 sts]
- Next row: P1, (p2tog) twice, P2, (ssp) twice, P1. [8 sts]
- Next row: K1, k2tog, K2, ssk, K1. [6 sts]
- Bind off pwise.

ARMS

Make 2

- Cast on 10 sts in purple.
- Work 22 rows in St st, beg with a K row.
- K 2 rows.
- Next row: Bind off 1 st, K to end.
- Rep last row once. [8 sts]
- Break yarn and join beige yarn.
- Work 3 rows in St st, beg with a K row.
- Next row: P4, m1 pwise, P4. [9 sts]
- Next row: K4, K into front and back of next st, turn and P these 2 sts, turn again, and K to end. [10 sts]

- Next row: P4, p2tog, P4. [9 sts]
- Next row: K4, k2tog, K3. [8 sts]
- Next row: p2tog, P to last 2 sts, p2tog. [6 sts]
- Bind off.

HAIR
Make 1
- Crochet a 3¼-inch (8-cm) chain in gray.

BEARD
Make 1
- Using size 1 (2.25 mm) needles, cast on 12 sts in gray, leaving a long tail (this will be used to crochet a short chain for one of the sideburns).
- 1st row: K.
- Next row: k2tog, K to last 2 sts, k2tog. [10 sts]
- Rep last row 4 times. [2 sts]
- Next row: k2tog, break yarn, leaving a long tail, and pull it through rem st.

With the yarn tail from casting on, crochet a ⅜-inch (1-cm) chain for the first sideburn. Thread the tail left over from binding off up the other side of the beard. Secure and crochet another ⅜-inch (1-cm) chain for the second sideburn.

MAKING UP
Fold the leg pieces in half lengthwise, so that the right side of your knitting is on the inside. Whipstitch the lower, back, and top parts of the feet. With the right sides of the two head pieces together, whipstitch around the edges. Turn the whole piece right side out. Sew the inside leg seams, shoulder seams, and one of the side seams of the sweater using mattress stitch, leaving one side of the sweater open for stuffing. Stuff Noah fairly firmly—especially his feet, because this will help him to stand up. Stitch the gap closed. Sew the arms in place so that the tops of the arms are level with the top neck edge of the sweater. For the sandals, work two big cross stitches on the top of the foot using dark brown yarn.

Using black yarn, make two French knots for the eyes. Using cream yarn, work a circle of chain stitches around each French knot.

For the mouth, separate a short length of red yarn into two thinner strands. Using one of these, embroider two straight stitches to form a V shape.

Use the red crayon to color the cheeks.

Arrange the hair chain in three small loops and sew them to the top of Noah's head. Sew the beard and sideburns around the lower half of the face.

APRON
The apron is worked in one piece, from the lower edge to the top.
Make 1
- Cast on 18 sts in orange.
- K 2 rows.
- Next and every ws row: K2, P to last 2 sts, K2.
- Next rs row: K.
- Next rs row: K.
- Next rs row: K.
- Next rs row: K.
- Next rs row: K5, put next 8 sts on a safety pin and keep on front of work, cast on 8 sts, K to end.
- Next rs row: K2, k2tog, K to last 4 sts, ssk, K2. [16 sts]
- Next rs row: K.
- Next rs row: K.
- Next rs row: K2, k2tog, K to last 4 sts, ssk, K2. [14 sts]
- Next rs row: K.
- Next rs row: K2, k2tog, K to last 4 sts, ssk, K2. [12 sts]
- Next rs row: K.
- Next rs row: K2, k2tog, K to last 4 sts, ssk, K2. [10 sts]
- Next rs row: K.
- K 3 rows.
- Bind off, leaving a long (12-inch/30-cm) tail; this will be used to create the apron neck loop.
- Pick up and K 8 sts from the safety pin on rs of work.
- Work 3 rows in St st, beg with a P row.
- K 2 rows.
- Bind off.

MAKING UP

Whipstitch the sides of the pocket in place. Use the yarn tail at the top corner of the apron to crochet a 2½-inch (6.5-cm) chain for the neck loop. Fasten the free end of the chain to the other side of the apron top. Work two 3¼-inch (8-cm) crochet chains for the waist ties. Attach these to the sides of the apron, level with the top of the pocket.

RAINCOAT

FRONT AND BACK

The front and back are worked as one piece.

Make 1

- Cast on 24 sts in bright yellow.
- K 12 rows.
- Next row: K2, P to last 2 sts, K2.
- Next row: K7, turn, leave rem sts on the stitch holder, and work on only these 7 sts.
- Next row: P5, K2.
- Next row: K.
- Rep these 2 rows twice.
- Break yarn and leave these 7 sts on a large safety pin.
- Rejoin yarn to the sts on the stitch holder with the rs facing you.
- Next row: K10, turn, leave rem sts on the stitch holder, and work on only these 10 sts.
- Work 7 rows in St st, beg with a K row.
- Break yarn and leave these 10 sts on a large safety pin.
- Rejoin yarn to 7 sts on the stitch holder with the rs facing you.
- Next row: K.
- Next row: K2, P5.
- Rep these 2 rows twice.
- Next row: K.
- Next row: K2, P5, P10 from next safety pin, then P5, K2 from the other safety pin. [24 sts]
- Next row: K.
- Next and every ws row: K2, P to last 2 sts, K2.
- Next rs row: K7, m1, K1, m1, K8, m1, K1, m1, K7. [28 sts]

- Next rs row: K.
- Next rs row: K8, m1, K1, m1, K10, m1, K1, m1, K8. [32 sts]
- Next rs row: K.
- Next rs row: K9, m1, K1, m1, K12, m1, K1, m1, K9. [36 sts]
- Next rs row: K.
- Next rs row: K10, m1, K1, m1, K14, m1, K1, m1, K10. [40 sts]
- Next rs row: K.
- Next rs row: K11, m1, K1, m1, K16, m1, K1, m1, K11. [44 sts]
- Next row: K2, P to last 2 sts, K2.
- Next row: K.
- Rep last 2 rows 4 times.
- K 5 rows.
- Bind off.

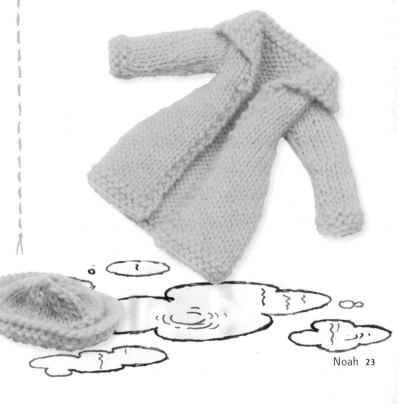

SLEEVES

The sleeves are worked from the shoulder edge to the wrist.

Make 2

- Cast on 16 sts in bright yellow.
- Work 10 rows in St st, beg with a K row.
- Next row: K2, k2tog, K8, ssk, K2. [14 sts]
- Work 7 rows in St st, beg with a P row.
- Next row: K2, k2tog, K6, ssk, K2. [12 sts]
- K 3 rows.
- Bind off.

BELT

Make 1

- Cast on 30 sts in bright yellow.
- K 1 row.
- Bind off.

MAKING UP

Sew the sleeve seams using mattress stitch, and whipstitch the sleeves to the armholes from the inside. Join the short edges of the belt and sew the button in place on the center front of the belt.

HAT

The hat is knitted as one piece, from the brim to the top.

Make 1

- Cast on 50 sts in bright yellow.
- K 3 rows.
- Next row: P.
- Next row: K2, (k2tog, K2) 12 times. [38 sts]
- Next row: P.
- Next row: K2, (k2tog, K2) 9 times. [29 sts]
- K 2 rows.
- Work 3 rows in St st, beg with a P row.
- Next row: K1, k2tog, (K3, k2tog) 5 times, K1. [23 sts]
- Next row: P1, (p2tog) 5 times, P1, (p2tog) 5 times, P1. [13 sts]
- Next row: (k2tog) 3 times, K1, (k2tog) 3 times. [7 sts]
- Break yarn and thread it through remaining sts.

MAKING UP

Pull the remaining stitches up fairly tightly and secure the yarn tail. Sew the back seam of the hat using mattress stitch.

BOOTS

Make 2

- Cast on 26 sts in olive green.
- Work 8 rows in St st, beg with a K row.
- Next row: K8, bind off 10 sts, K to end. [16 sts]
- Work 6 rows in St st, beg with a P row.
- Bind off kwise fairly loosely.

MAKING UP

Fold the boots in half so that the right side of your knitting is on the inside. Whipstitch the lower and top seams of the boots. Turn the boots right side out and sew the back seam using mattress stitch.

Mrs. Noah

The Bible never refers to Noah's wife by her first name, so she's usually simply known as "Mrs. Noah." She wears a practical pinafore-style dress over a simple sweater, but, like her husband, she is ready for stormy weather and has a jaunty rain hat to protect her flecked-gray hair, a practical rain cape, and some sturdy black rubber boots on standby.

You will need

FOR THE DOLL

3/8 oz./9 g (24 yd./22 m) of beige DK yarn

1/4 oz./6 g (15 yd./14 m) of bright pink DK yarn

1/8 oz./3 g (7 yd./6 m) of flecked-gray DK yarn

A small amount of pale pink DK yarn

Very small amounts of black, cream, and red DK yarn

3/4 oz./20 g of polyester toy filling

A red crayon for coloring the cheeks

FOR THE CLOTHES

1/4 oz./7 g (19 yd./17 m) of turquoise DK yarn

1/2 oz./12 g (32 yd./29 m) of lime green DK yarn

1/8 oz./4 g (11 yd./10 m) of red DK yarn

1/4 oz./5 g (13 yd./12 m) of black DK yarn

Use size 2/3 (3 mm) knitting needles and a size D-3 (3.25 mm) crochet hook

DOLL

LEGS, BODY, AND HEAD

Mrs. Noah's legs, body, and head are knitted as one piece, from the feet upward. The bright pink sweater and pale pink pants are knitted as part of the doll.

Make 1

- Cast on 22 sts in beige for the first foot.
- Work 6 rows in St st, beg with a K row.
- Next row: K6, bind off 10 sts, K to end. [12 sts]
- Work 15 rows in St st, beg with a P row.
- Break yarn and leave sts on a spare needle or stitch holder.
- Work the second foot and leg in exactly the same way.
- Break yarn and join pale pink yarn.
- Next row: K9 across second leg, put last 3 sts on a safety pin.
- On first leg, put first 3 sts on a safety pin, K6, put last 3 sts on a safety pin.
- Next row: K to last 3 sts, put these 3 sts on a safety pin.
- Work on the 12 sts remaining on the needle.
- Work 6 rows in St st, beg with a K row.
- * Break yarn and join bright pink yarn.
- K 4 rows.
- Work 10 rows in St st, beg with a K row.
- Next row: Bind off 2 sts, K to end.
- Rep last row once. [8 sts]
- Break yarn.
- Rejoin beige yarn.
- Work 2 rows in St st, beg with a K row.
- Next row: (K1, m1) twice, K4, (m1, K1) twice. [12 sts]
- Next row: P.
- Next row: (K1, m1) 3 times, K6, (m1, K1) 3 times. [18 sts]
- Next row: P.
- Next row: K2, m1, K14, m1, K2. [20 sts] **
- Next row: P10, m1 pwise, P10. [21 sts]

- Next row: K10, K into front and back of made st, turn work and P these 2 sts, turn work again, and K to end. [22 sts]
- Next row: P9, p2tog, ssp, P9. [20 sts]
- Next row: K8, k2tog, ssk, K8. [18 sts]
- Next row: P.
- Next row: K2, (k2tog) 3 times, K2, (ssk) 3 times, K2. [12 sts]
- Next row: P1, (p2tog) twice, P2, (ssp) twice, P1. [8 sts]
- Next row: K1, k2tog, K2, ssk, K1. [6 sts]
- Bind off pwise.

- With pale pink yarn and with ws of work facing you, pick up and P 12 sts across back of legs.
- Work 6 rows in St st, beg with a K row.
- Work as for front side from * to **.
- Next row: P.
- Next row: K.
- Rep last 2 rows once.
- Next row: p2tog, P to last 2 sts, p2tog. [18 sts]
- Next row: K2, (k2tog) 3 times, K2, (ssk) 3 times, K2. [12 sts]
- Next row: P1, (p2tog) twice, P2, (ssp) twice, P1. [8 sts]
- Next row: K1, k2tog, K2, ssk, K1. [6 sts]
- Bind off pwise.

ARMS

Make 2

- Cast on 10 sts in bright pink.
- Work 18 rows in St st, beg with a K row.
- K 2 rows.
- Next row: Bind off 1 st, K to end.
- Rep last row once. [8 sts]
- Break yarn and join beige yarn.
- Work 3 rows in St st, beg with a K row.
- Next row: P4, m1 pwise, P4. [9 sts]
- Next row: K4, K into front and back of next st, turn work and P these 2 sts, turn work again, and K to end. [10 sts]
- Next row: P4, p2tog, P4. [9 sts]
- Next row: K4, k2tog, K3. [8 sts]
- Next row: p2tog, P to last 2 sts, p2tog. [6 sts]
- Bind off firmly.

HAIR

Make 1

- Cast on 18 sts in flecked gray.
- Work 10 rows in St st, beg with a K row.
- Next row: Bind off 4 sts, K to end. [14 sts]
- Next row: Bind off 4 sts pwise, P to end. [10 sts]
- Work 9 rows in St st, beg with a K row.
- Bind off pwise.

MAKING UP

Fold the leg pieces in half lengthwise so that the right side of your knitting is on the inside. Whipstitch the lower, back, and top parts of the feet. With the right sides of the two head pieces together, whipstitch around the edges. Turn the whole piece right side out. Sew the inside leg seams, shoulder seams, and one of the side seams of the sweater using mattress stitch, leaving one side of the sweater open for stuffing. Stuff fairly firmly to help her stand up, then stitch the gap closed. Sew the arms in place so that the tops of the arms are level with the top neck edge of the sweater.

Fold the edges of the hair piece upward and whipstitch the seams from the inside to form a box shape with one short side. The right side should be on the outside of the box shape. Whipstitch the hair in place on top of the head.

Using black yarn, make two French knots for the eyes. Using cream yarn, work a circle of chain stitches around each French knot. Using a single strand of black yarn, work three small straight stitches above each eye for the eyelashes.

For the mouth, separate a short length of red yarn into two thinner strands. Using one of these, embroider two straight stitches to form a V shape.

Use the red crayon to color the cheeks.

DRESS

The dress is worked in one piece, beginning at the lower edge of the front.

Make 1

- Cast on 18 sts in turquoise.
- Work 3 rows in St st, beg with a P row.
- K 2 rows.
- Work 4 rows in St st, beg with a K row.
- Next row: K1, k2tog, K12, ssk, K1. [16 sts]
- Work 5 rows in St st, beg with a P row.
- Next row: K1, k2tog, K10, ssk, K1. [14 sts]
- Work 5 rows in St st, beg with a P row.
- Next row: (K1, P1) to end.
- Next row: (P1, K1) to end.
- Rep last 2 rows twice.
- Next row: (K1, P1) twice, bind off 6 sts keeping to K1, P1 pattern (1 st on needle after binding off), P1, K1, P1. [4 sts]
- Work on only 4 sts just worked.
- Next row: (P1, K1) twice.
- Next row: (K1, P1) twice.
- Rep last 2 rows 3 times.
- Next row: (P1, K1) twice.
- Break yarn and rejoin it to the neck edge of the other side of the dress on the ws of the work.
- Next row: (P1, K1) twice.
- Next row: (K1, P1) twice.
- Rep last 2 rows twice more.
- Next row: (P1, K1) twice.
- Next row: (K1, P1) twice, cast on 6 sts, (K1, P1) twice. [14 sts]
- Next row: (P1, K1) to end.

- Next row: (K1, P1) to end.
- Rep last 2 rows twice.
- Next row: (P1, K1) to end.
- Work 4 rows in St st, beg with a K row.
- Next row: K1, m1, K12, m1, K1. [16 sts]
- Work 5 rows in St st, beg with a P row.
- Next row: K1, m1, K14, m1, K1. [18 sts]
- Work 4 rows in St st, beg with a P row
- Next row: K.
- Work 3 rows in St st, beg with a K row.
- Bind off pwise.

MAKING UP

With the right sides facing outward and using mattress stitch, sew the side seams from the lower edge to the beginning of the seed-stitch yoke.

RAIN CAPE

The rain cape is knitted as one piece from the neck to the lower edge.

Make 1

- Cast on 22 sts in lime green, leaving a long tail; this will be used to crochet a chain for one of the neck ties.
- K 3 rows.
- Next row: K5, m1, K1, m1, K10, m1, K1, m1, K5. [26 sts]
- Next and every ws row: K2, P to last 2 sts, K2.
- Next rs row: K6, m1, K1, m1, K12, m1, K1, m1, K6. [30 sts]
- Next rs row: K7, m1, K1, m1, K14, m1, K1, m1, K7. [34 sts]
- Next rs row: K8, m1, K1, m1, K16, m1, K1, m1, K8. [38 sts]
- Next rs row: K9, m1, K1, m1, K18, m1, K1, m1, K9. [42 sts]
- Next rs row: K10, m1, K1, m1, K20, m1, K1, m1, K10. [46 sts]
- Next rs row: K11, m1, K1, m1, K22, m1, K1, m1, K11. [50 sts]
- Work 18 rows in St st beg with a P row, remembering to K2 sts at the beg and end of every ws row.
- Next row: K.
- Bind off.

MAKING UP

Use the neck-edge yarn tail to crochet a 1½-inch (4-cm) chain for one of the neck ties. Make another crochet chain to match and attach it to the other neck edge. On each front side of the cape, work a short row of chain stitch diagonally to represent the pockets.

HAT

Make 1

- Cast on 30 sts in red.
- Work 6 rows in St st, beg with a K row.
- Next row: Bind off 12 sts, K6, bind off 12 sts.
- Break yarn and with ws facing you, rejoin yarn to rem 6 sts.
- Next row: P.
- Next row: K1, m1, K to last 2 sts, m1, K1. [8 sts]
- Next row: P.
- Rep last 2 rows once. [10 sts]
- Work 2 rows in St st, beg with a K row.
- Next row: K1, ssk, K4, k2tog, K1. [8 sts]
- Next row: P.
- Next row: K1, ssk, K2, k2tog, K1. [6 sts]
- Bind off pwise.
- With rs of the top part of the hat facing you, pick up and K 30 sts along cast-on edge.
- Next row: P.
- Next row: K1, (inc1) 28 times, K1. [58 sts]
- Work 3 rows in St st beg with a P row.
- Bind off loosely.

MAKING UP

Join the back seam of the hat using mattress stitch and whipstitch the top part of the hat to the top of the side band from the inside.

BOOTS

Make 2

- Cast on 24 sts in black.
- Work 8 rows in St st, beg with a K row.
- Next row: K8, bind off 8 sts, K to end. [16 sts]
- Work 6 rows in St st, beg with a P row.
- Bind off kwise fairly loosely.

MAKING UP

Fold the boots in half so that the right side of your knitting is on the inside. Whipstitch the lower and top seams of the boots. Turn the boots right side out and sew the back seam using mattress stitch.

Noah Rounds Up the Animals

While they worked, Noah kept worrying about how his family would live in a world that had no other people and no animals, apart from creatures that could live in the ocean such as fish. What would such a world be like?

God had thought of that, however. When the work on the Ark was finished, He came to Noah with more instructions: "Collect seven of every kind of clean animal"—by that He meant the kind of animal that we eat, such as chickens and sheep—"and two of every kind of unclean animal"—He meant bears and monkeys and crocodiles, the kind we don't eat. "Choose a male and female of each, so that the species will survive. You must also find enough food for all of them. Be warned: The rains are going to fall for forty days and forty nights."

Once again Noah obeyed. As you can imagine, it took him a long time to collect all the animals in the world. It was especially difficult to capture the birds because they kept flying off, but eventually, by the time he was six hundred years old, he had two of each of the unclean creatures that lived on the earth and seven of each of the clean ones, with a male and a female of every species. He gathered them all by the Ark and waited for God to tell him what to do next.

Elephants

Elephants are the largest land mammals on the planet and can weigh several tons. They use their trunks for smelling, as you would expect, but also for grabbing things and cooling themselves down with squirts of water. This woolly pair are made from a smooth gray yarn. You'll find them almost as lovable as the real thing.

You will need

FOR BOTH ELEPHANTS

2 oz./56 g (137 yd./125 m) of medium gray DK yarn

Very small amounts of cream and black DK yarn

2⅛ oz./60 g of polyester toy filling

Use size 2/3 (3 mm) knitting needles, except when instructed to use size 2 (2.75 mm) knitting needles

SHE ELEPHANT
BODY, HEAD, AND TRUNK
The body, head, and trunk are knitted as one piece.
Make 1
- Cast on 38 sts in medium gray.
- 1st row: K18, inc1, K19. [39 sts]
- Next row: P19, m1, inc1 pwise, P19. [41 sts]
- Next row: K20, m1, K1, m1, K20. [43 sts]
- Work 31 rows in St st, beg with a P row.
- Next row: Bind off 10 sts, K6 (incl st on needle from binding off), (m1, K1) 11 times, m1, K to end. [45 sts]
- Next row: Bind off 10 sts pwise, P to end. [35 sts]
- Next row: K2, k2tog, K to last 4 sts, ssk, K2. [33 sts]
- Next row: P.
- Rep last 2 rows 4 times. [25 sts]
- Next row: K2, k2tog, K1, k2tog, K11, s1, K1, psso, K1, s1, K1, psso, K2. [21 sts]
- Next and every ws row: P.
- Next rs row: K2, k2tog, K1, k2tog, K7, s1, K1, psso, K1, s1, K1, psso, K2. [17 sts]
- Next rs row: K2, k2tog, K1, k2tog, K3, s1, K1, psso, K1, s1, K1, psso, K2. [13 sts]
- Work 7 rows in St st, beg with a P row.
- Next row: K2, k2tog, K5, ssk, K2. [11 sts]
- Work 7 rows in St st, beg with a P row.
- Next row: K2, k2tog, K3, ssk, K2. [9 sts]
- Work 9 rows in St st, beg with a P row.
- Bind off.

LEGS
Make 4
- Cast on 12 sts in medium gray.
- K 5 rows.
- Work 16 rows in St st, beg with a K row.
- Bind off.

EARS
The ears are knitted from the inside to the outside edge.
Make 2
- Cast on 6 sts in medium gray.
- 1st row: inc1, K to last 2 sts, inc1, K1. [8 sts]
- Next row: K.
- Next row: K1, m1, K to last st, m1, K1. [10 sts]
- Next row: K.
- Rep last 2 rows 4 times. [18 sts]
- Next row: k2tog, K to last 2 sts, ssk. [16 sts]
- Rep last row once. [14 sts]
- Bind off.

TAIL
Make 1
- Cast on 12 sts in medium gray.
- K 1 row.
- Bind off.

HE ELEPHANT
BODY, HEAD, AND TRUNK
The body, head, and trunk are knitted as one piece.
Make 1
- Cast on 42 sts in medium gray.
- 1st row: K20, inc1, K21. [43 sts]
- Next row: P21, m1, inc1 pwise, P21. [45 sts]
- Next row: K22, m1, K1, m1, K22. [47 sts]
- Work 35 rows in St st, beg with a P row.
- Next row: Bind off 11 sts, K7 (incl st on needle from binding off), (m1, K1) 11 times, m1, K to end. [48 sts]
- Next row: Bind off 11 sts pwise, P to end. [37 sts]
- Next row: K2, k2tog, K to last 4 sts, ssk, K2. [35 sts]
- Next row: P.
- Rep last 2 rows 4 times. [27 sts]
- Next row: K2, k2tog, K1, k2tog, K13, s1, K1, psso, K1, s1, K1, psso, K2. [23 sts]
- Next and every ws row: P.
- Next rs row: K2, k2tog, K1, k2tog, K9, s1, K1, psso, K1, s1, K1, psso, K2. [19 sts]

- **Next rs row:** K2, k2tog, K1, k2tog, K5, s1, K1, psso, K1, s1, K1, psso, K2. [15 sts]
- **Work 7 rows in St st, beg with a P row.**
- **Next row:** K2, k2tog, K7, ssk, K2. [13 sts]
- **Work 7 rows in St st, beg with a P row.**
- **Next row:** K2, k2tog, K5, ssk, K2. [11 sts]
- **Work 7 rows in St st, beg with a P row.**
- **Next row:** K2, k2tog, K3, ssk, K2. [9 sts]
- **Work 5 rows in St st, beg with a P row.**
- **Bind off.**

LEGS
Make 4
- **Cast on 14 sts in medium gray.**
- **K 5 rows.**
- **Work 18 rows in St st.**
- **Bind off.**

EARS
Work as for the She Elephant.

TAIL
Make 1
- **Cast on 15 sts in medium gray.**
- **K 1 row.**
- **Bind off.**

TUSKS
Make 2
- **Using size 2 (2.75 mm) needles, cast on 13 sts in cream.**
- **Bind off.**

MAKING UP
Fold the body piece in half to form the elephant shape. Using mattress stitch, seam the piece on the underside of the trunk and body, leaving the back open for stuffing. Stuff the elephant, then close the gap using mattress stitch.

Seam the legs using mattress stitch. Stuff the legs and whipstitch them in place. The seams should run up the insides of the legs.

Position the ears facedown on the elephant and whipstitch them in place so that your stitching is on the back edge of the ears.

Sew the tail in place.

For the He Elephant tusks, zigzag one of the yarn tails down the outer edges of the tusk pieces, pulling the yarn up firmly every few stitches to form a dense cord. Thread the other yarn tail down the length of the tusk, pulling it tightly to form the tusk into a slight curve. Whipstitch the tusks in place.

Using black yarn, work two French knots for the eyes. Using cream yarn, work a circle of chain stitch around each French knot. For the She Elephant, using a single strand of black yarn, work three small straight stitches above each eye for the eyelashes.

Using black yarn, work a straight stitch for the mouth, just underneath the trunk.

Lions

This King of Beasts probably made sure that he and his better half were among the first passengers onboard the Ark. These lions are much more gentle than most, which is excellent news for the other passengers, many of whom would make a tasty morsel for the average hungry pair of great cats.

You will need

FOR BOTH LIONS

1¼ oz./35 g (94 yd./86 m) of pale yellow DK yarn

A small amount of mustard DK yarn

Very small amounts of black, cream, and dark gray DK yarn

1½ oz./40 g of polyester toy filling

Use size 2/3 (3 mm) knitting needles and a size D-3 (3.25 mm) crochet hook

SHE LION

BODY
Make 1
- Cast on 24 sts in pale yellow.
- Work 4 rows in St st, beg with a K row.
- Next row: K2, m1, K to last 2 sts, m1, K2. [26 sts]
- Work 5 rows in St st, beg with a P row.
- Rep last 6 rows 3 times. [32 sts]
- Next row: Bind off 5 sts, K to end. [27 sts]
- Next row: Bind off 5 sts, P to end. [22 sts]
- Bind off.

LEGS
Make 4
- Cast on 12 sts in pale yellow.
- Work 16 rows in St st, beg with a K row.
- Bind off.

HEAD

Both head pieces are worked from the bottom of the jaw to the top of the head.

FRONT
Make 1

- Cast on 6 sts in pale yellow.
- Work 2 rows in St st, beg with a K row.
- Next row: (K1, m1) twice, K2, (m1, K1) twice. [10 sts]
- Next and every ws row: P.
- Next rs row: (K1, m1) twice, K6, (m1, K1) twice. [14 sts]
- Next rs row: K6, m1, K2, m1, K6. [16 sts]
- Next rs row: K6, m1, K4, m1, K6. [18 sts]
- Next rs row: K.
- Next rs row: K5, k2tog, K4, ssk, K5. [16 sts] *
- Next rs row: K5, k2tog, K2, ssk, K5. [14 sts]
- Next rs row: K5, k2tog, ssk, K5. [12 sts]
- Next rs row: K2, (k2tog) twice, (ssk) twice, K2. [8 sts]
- Bind off pwise.

BACK
Make 1

- Work as for front of head to *.
- Next row: P.
- Next rs row: K4, k2tog, K4, ssk, K4. [14 sts]
- Next rs row: K3, k2tog, K4, ssk, K3. [12 sts]
- Next rs row: K1, (k2tog) twice, K2, (ssk) twice, K1. [8 sts]
- Bind off pwise.

EARS
Make 2

- Cast on 5 sts in pale yellow.
- Work 2 rows in St st, beg with a K row.
- Next row: k2tog, K1, ssk. [3 sts]
- Next row: P.
- Next row: K1, m1, K1, m1, K1. [5 sts]
- Work 3 rows in St st, beg with a P row.
- Bind off.

TAIL
Make 1

- Cast on 22 sts in pale yellow.
- Bind off.

For the switch, using mustard yarn, crochet a 5½-inch (14-cm) chain. Arrange the chain in three small loops and sew to the end of the tail.

HE LION

BODY
Make 1

- Cast on 24 sts in pale yellow.
- Work 4 rows in St st, beg with a K row.
- Next row: K2, m1, K to last 2 sts, m1, K1. [26 sts]
- Work 5 rows in St st, beg with a P row.
- Rep last 6 rows once more. [28 sts]
- Next row: K2, m1, K to last 2 sts, m1, K2. [30 sts]
- Work 3 rows in St st, beg with a P row.
- Rep last 4 rows 3 times more. [36 sts]
- Work 2 rows in St st, beg with a K row.
- Next row: Bind off 4 sts, K to end. [32 sts]
- Next row: Bind off 4 sts, P to end. [28 sts]
- Bind off.

LEGS
Make 4

- Cast on 13 sts in pale yellow.
- Work 18 rows in St st, beg with a K row.
- Bind off.

HEAD

Both head pieces are worked from the bottom of the jaw to the top of the head.

FRONT
Make 1

- Cast on 8 sts in pale yellow.
- Work 2 rows in St st, beg with a K row.
- Next row: (K1, m1) twice, K4, (m1, K1) twice. [12 sts]
- Next and every ws row: P.

- **Next rs row: (K1, m1) twice, K8, (m1, K1) twice. [16 sts]**
- **Next rs row: K7, m1, K2, m1, K7. [18 sts]**
- **Next rs row: K7, m1, K4, m1, K7. [20 sts]**
- **Next rs row: K8, m1, K4, m1, K8. [22 sts]**
- **Next rs row: K7, k2tog, K4, ssk, K7. [20 sts] ***
- **Next rs row: K7, k2tog, K2, ssk, K7. [18 sts]**
- **Next rs row: K7, k2tog, ssk, K7. [16 sts]**
- **Next rs row: K6, k2tog, ssk, K6. [14 sts]**
- **Next rs row: K2, (k2tog) twice, K2, (ssk) twice, K2. [10 sts]**
- **Bind off pwise.**

BACK
Make 1
- **Work as for front of head to *.**
- **Next row: P.**
- **Next rs row: K6, k2tog, K4, ssk, K6. [18 sts]**
- **Next rs row: K5, k2tog, K4, ssk, K5. [16 sts]**
- **Next rs row: K4, k2tog, K4, ssk, K4. [14 sts]**
- **Next rs row: K2, (k2tog) twice, K2, (ssk) twice, K2. [10 sts]**
- **Bind off pwise.**

MANE
Using mustard yarn, crochet a 6¼-inch (16-cm) chain. The individual stitches should be fairly loose (about ¼ inch/5 mm across). Now work 7 stitches, then use your crochet hook to join the last of these stitches to the first. Work another 7 stitches, then join the last stitch to the next stitch along on the original chain. Continue in this way until you have a series of loops along the length of the chain.

EARS
Work as for the She Lion.

TAIL
Work as for the She Lion.

MAKING UP
Place the two head pieces right sides together and whipstitch around the edge, leaving a gap at the lower edge. Turn the head right side out through this gap, stuff the head, and close the gap.

Using mattress stitch, join the lower and back seams of the body piece, leaving the neck end open. Stuff the body. Whipstitch the neck edge to the back of the head, so that the neck forms a circle on the back of the head.

Seam the legs using mattress stitch. Stuff the legs and whipstitch them in place. The seams should run up the insides of the legs.

Fold the ear pieces so that the right side is on the inside and whipstitch around the curved edges. Turn the ears right side out and sew them in place.

Sew the mane in position on the He Lion.

Sew the tail in position.

Using black yarn, work two French knots for the eyes. Using cream yarn, work a circle of chain stitch around each French knot. For the She Lion, using a single strand of black yarn, work three small straight stitches above each eye for the eyelashes.

Using dark gray yarn, work the noses in satin stitch and the mouths in back stitch.

The Animals Go in Two by Two

Once Noah had collected all the animals, God said, "Now it is time to bring your family and all the animals onto the Ark."

Noah began to drive the animals, two by two, up the gangplank. Unclean beasts were shown to the top level of the Ark; clean beasts and Noah's own family would live on the second level; and the lowest level would be used for waste.

As he worked, Noah's neighbors stood laughing and pointing at the spectacle. "He thinks there will be forty days and forty nights of rain," they laughed. "He must be crazy."

They lived in an area where it hardly ever rained—the most moisture they ever had was dew on the ground in the morning—so no one thought it could possibly be true.

Noah believed it, though, because he had heard it directly from God. "Come with us," he offered. "Save yourselves." But no one else would come.

Once he had finished loading all the animals, Noah boarded the Ark along with his wife and his three sons and their three wives, and they pulled up the gangplank behind them.

Noah and his family and all the animals lived on the Ark for seven days, but nothing happened. The skies were clear and sunny, and there was no sign of

rain. Noah's neighbors continued to shout insults. "You see? You were wrong," they shouted with glee.

But suddenly, toward the end of the seventh day, God caused the door of the Ark to slam shut with a loud crashing sound. Up above, the skies darkened, and the air grew chilly. And then the first drop of rain fell.

Monkeys

These monkeys like nothing better than . . . you've guessed it . . . monkeying around—and eating bananas, of course. They're agile and crazy, so it will probably be the monkeys' job to entertain the other passengers on the Ark. You can conceal a short length of wire in the monkeys' tails to help them dangle from the Ark's rafters.

You will need

FOR BOTH MONKEYS

¾ oz./20 g (55 yd./50 m) of pale gray DK yarn

A small amount of caramel DK yarn for the She Monkey and a small amount of cream DK yarn for the He Monkey

Very small amounts of black, cream, and red DK yarn

½ oz./15 g of polyester toy filling

Two short lengths of covered garden wire or chenille sticks for the inside of the tails (optional)

Use size 2/3 (3 mm) knitting needles, except when instructed to use size 1 (2.25 mm) knitting needles

SHE AND HE MONKEYS

The He Monkey with the cream muzzle has a slightly longer body and tail than the She Monkey with the caramel muzzle. The pattern includes the slight variation needed to knit both monkeys.

BODY AND HEAD

Make 2

- Cast on 8 sts in pale gray.
- Work 2 rows in St st, beg with a K row.
- Next row: K2, m1, K to last 2 sts, m1, K2. [10 sts]
- Next row: P.
- Rep last 2 rows twice. [14 sts]

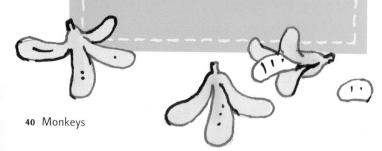

- For the She Monkey, work 3 rows in St st, beg with a P row.
- For the He Monkey, work 5 rows in St st, beg with a P row.
- Next row: K3, k2tog, K4, ssk, K3. [12 sts]
- Next and every ws row: P.
- Next rs row: K3, k2tog, K2, ssk, K3. [10 sts]
- Next rs row: K3, k2tog, ssk, K3. [8 sts]
- Next rs row: (K1, m1) twice, K4, (m1, K1) twice. [12 sts]
- Next rs row: K1, m1, K10, m1, K1. [14 sts]
- Next rs row: K4, m1, K6, m1, K4. [16 sts]
- Next rs row: K4, m1, K8, m1, K4. [18 sts]
- Next rs row: K4, k2tog, K6, ssk, K4. [16 sts]
- Next rs row: K4, (k2tog) twice, (ssk) twice, K4. [12 sts]
- Next rs row: K2, (k2tog) twice, (ssk) twice, K2. [8 sts]
- Bind off pwise.

MUZZLE
Make 1
- For the She Monkey, cast on 6 sts in caramel.
- For the He Monkey, cast on 6 sts in cream.
- Next row: inc1, K3, inc1, K1. [8 sts]
- K 2 rows.
- Next row: K1, k2tog, K2, ssk, K1. [6 sts]
- Next row: K.
- Bind off.

ARMS AND LEGS
Make 4
- Cast on 6 sts in pale gray.
- Work 17 rows in St st, beg with a K row.
- Next row: P3, m1 pwise, P3. [7 sts]
- Next row: K3, K into front and back of next st, turn work and P2, turn work again, and K to end. [8 sts]
- Next row: P3, p2tog, P3. [7 sts]
- Work 2 rows in St st, beg with a K row.
- Next row: k2tog, K3, ssk. [5 sts]
- Bind off pwise.

EARS
Make 2
- Using size 1 (2.25 mm) needles, cast on 5 sts in pale gray.
- K2 rows.
- Next row: k2tog, K1, ssk. [3 sts]
- Next row: s1, k2tog, psso. [1 st]
- Break yarn and pull it through rem st.

TAIL
Make 1
- For the She Monkey, cast on 25 sts in pale gray.
- For the He Monkey, cast on 30 sts in pale gray.
- K 1 row.
- Bind off.

MAKING UP
Place the two body and head pieces right sides together and whipstitch around the outside, leaving the lower edge open for turning and stuffing. Turn the piece right side out, stuff, and sew the gap closed.

Seam the arms and legs using mattress stitch and whipstitch them in position.

Whipstitch the ears in place.

Whipstitch the long sides of the tail together. If you are using wire in the tail, trap the wire in the tail as you sew. Sew the tail in place at the back of the body so that the tail points upward.

Divide a strand of black yarn into two lengthwise and use one of these to work two French knots for the eyes. Using cream yarn, work a circle of chain stitches around each French knot. Using a single strand of black yarn, work a few straight stitches above the eyes of the She Monkey for the eyelashes.

Whipstitch the muzzle to the face so that the bound-off edge forms the lower edge of the muzzle. In the first "groove" between the two rows of stitches at the bottom of the muzzle, work the mouth in chain stitch, using red yarn for the She Monkey and black yarn for the He Monkey. Using a single strand of black yarn, work two French knots for the nostrils.

Tigers

Tigers are the biggest cats in the world and probably the fiercest—except for this pair, of course, which really are just big pussycats. This stripy pair is knitted in two slightly different shades of burnt orange, but you could just as easily use one shade for your own snarling twosome.

SHE TIGER
BODY
Make 1
- Cast on 24 sts in burnt orange.
- Work 4 rows in St st, beg with a K row.
- Leave burnt orange yarn at side and join black yarn.
- Work 2 rows in St st, beg with a K row.
- Leave black yarn at side and use burnt orange yarn.
- Next row: K2, m1, K to last 2 sts, m1, K2. [26 sts]
- Work 3 rows in St st, beg with a P row.
- In black yarn, work 2 rows in St st, beg with a K row.
- Rep last 6 rows twice more. [30 sts]
- Break black yarn.
- In burnt orange yarn, work 2 rows in St st, beg with a K row.
- Next row: Bind off 5 sts, K to end. [25 sts]
- Next row: Bind off 5 sts pwise, P to end. [20 sts]
- Bind off.

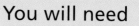

You will need

FOR BOTH TIGERS

1⅛ oz./32 g (85 yd./78 m) of burnt orange DK yarn

⅛ oz./4 g (11 yd./10 m) of black DK yarn

Very small amounts of white and pale pink DK yarn

1 oz./30 g of polyester toy filling

Use size 2/3 (3 mm) knitting needles

HEAD

Both head pieces are worked from the bottom of the jaw to the top of the head.

FRONT

Make 1

- Cast on 6 sts in burnt orange.
- Work 2 rows in St st, beg with a K row.
- Next row: (K1, m1) twice, K2, (m1, K1) twice. [10 sts]
- Next and every ws row: P.
- Next rs row: (K1, m1) twice, K6, (m1, K1) twice. [14 sts]
- Next rs row: K.
- Next rs row: K6, m1, K2, m1, K6. [16 sts]
- Next rs row: K6, m1, K4, m1, K6. [18 sts]
- Next rs row: K5, k2tog, K4, ssk, K5. [16 sts] *
- Next rs row: K5, k2tog, K2, ssk, K5. [14 sts]
- Next rs row: K5, k2tog, ssk, K5. [12 sts]
- Next rs row: K2, (k2tog) twice, (ssk) twice, K2. [8 sts]
- Bind off pwise.

BACK

Make 1

- Work as for front of head to *.
- Next row: P.
- Next rs row: K4, k2tog, K4, ssk, K4. [14 sts]
- Next rs row: K3, k2tog, K4, ssk, K3. [12 sts]
- Next rs row: K1, (k2tog) twice, K2, (ssk) twice, K1. [8 sts]
- Bind off pwise.

EARS

Make 2

- Cast on 5 sts in burnt orange.
- Work 2 rows in St st, beg with a K row.
- Next row: k2tog, K1, ssk. [3 sts]
- Next row: P.
- Next row: K1, m1, K1, m1, K1. [5 sts]
- Work 3 rows in St st, beg with a P row.
- Bind off.

LEGS

Make 4

- Cast on 12 sts in burnt orange.
- Work 14 rows in St st, beg with a K row.
- Bind off.

TAIL

Make 1

- Cast on 18 sts in burnt orange.
- K 1 row.
- Bind off.

HE TIGER

BODY

Make 1

- Cast on 26 sts in burnt orange.
- Work 4 rows in St st, beg with a K row.
- Leave burnt orange yarn at side and join black yarn.
- Work 2 rows in St st, beg with a K row.
- Leave black yarn at side and use burnt orange yarn.
- Next row: K2, m1, K to last 2 sts, m1, K2. [28 sts]
- Work 3 rows in St st, beg with a P row.
- In black yarn, work 2 rows in St st, beg with a K row.
- Rep last 6 rows 3 times. [34 sts]
- Break black yarn.
- In burnt orange yarn, work 2 rows in St st, beg with a K row.
- Next row: Bind off 5 sts, K to end. [29 sts]
- Next row: Bind off 5 sts pwise, P to end. [24 sts]
- Bind off.

HEAD

Both head pieces are worked from the bottom of the jaw to the top of the head.

FRONT

Make 1

- Cast on 6 sts in burnt orange.
- Work 2 rows in St st, beg with a K row.
- Next row: (K1, m1) twice, K2, (m1, K1) twice. [10 sts]

- Next and every ws row: P.
- Next rs row: (K1, m1) twice, K6, (m1, K1) twice. [14 sts]
- Next rs row: K.
- Next rs row: K6, m1, K2, m1, K6. [16 sts]
- Next rs row: K6, m1, K4, m1, K6. [18 sts]
- Next rs row: K.
- Next rs row: K5, k2tog, K4, ssk, K5. [16 sts] *
- Next rs row: K5, k2tog, K2, ssk, K5. [14 sts]
- Next rs row: K5, k2tog, ssk, K5. [12 sts]
- Next rs row: K2, (k2tog) twice, (ssk) twice, K2. [8 sts]
- Bind off pwise.

BACK
Make 1
- Work as for front of head to *.
- Next row: P.
- Next rs row: K4, k2tog, K4, ssk, K4. [14 sts]
- Next rs row: K3, k2tog, K4, ssk, K3. [12 sts]
- Next rs row: K1, (k2tog) twice, K2, (ssk) twice, K1. [8 sts]
- Bind off pwise.

EARS
Work as for the She Tiger.

LEGS
Make 4
- Cast on 13 sts in burnt orange.
- Work 16 rows in St st, beg with a K row.
- Bind off.

TAIL
Work as for the She Tiger.

MAKING UP
Place the two head pieces right sides together and whipstitch around the edge, leaving a gap at the lower edge. Turn the head right side out through this gap, stuff the head, and close the gap.

Using mattress stitch, join the lower and back seams of the body piece, leaving the neck end open. Stuff the body. Whipstitch the neck edge to the back of the head, so that the neck forms a circle on the back of the head.

Seam the legs using mattress stitch. Stuff the legs and whipstitch them in place. The seams should run down the insides of the legs.

Fold the ear pieces so that the right side is on the inside and whipstitch around the curved edges. Turn the ears right side out and sew them in place.

Whipstitch the long sides of the tail together in the way the piece naturally curls. Sew the tail in position.

Using black yarn, work two French knots for the eyes. Using white yarn, work a circle of chain stitches around each French knot. For the She Tiger, using a single strand of black yarn, work a few straight stitches above each eye for the eyelashes.

Work the nose in satin stitch using black yarn. For the He Tiger, work the mouth in straight stitch using black yarn. For the She Tiger's mouth, work a ring of chain stitches in black yarn. Work a row of chain stitches in white yarn for the teeth and work a few chain stitches in pale pink for the inside of the mouth. Using black yarn, work the markings on the cheeks and down the top of the head in chain stitch.

Crocodiles

These knobby-backed reptiles are re-created in wool using a version of seed stitch and a dark green yarn. With their long snouts and chain stitch smiles, you won't mind getting up close to this snappy couple.

SHE AND HE CROCODILES

The snout and body of the He Crocodile is slightly longer than that of the She Crocodile. The pattern includes the slight variation needed to knit both animals.

UPPER BODY
Make 1

- Cast on 7 sts in bottle green.
- 1st row: K1, k2tog, K1, ssk, K1. [5 sts]
- Next row: P.
- Next row: inc1, K2, inc1, K1. [7 sts]
- For the She Crocodile, work 3 rows in St st, beg with a P row.
- For the He Crocodile, work 5 rows in St st, beg with a P row.
- Next row: inc1, K to last 2 sts, inc1, K1. [9 sts]
- Next row: P.
- Rep last 2 rows once. [11 sts]
- Work 6 rows in St st, beg with a K row.
- Next row: K1, (k2tog) twice, K1, (ssk) twice, K1. [7 sts]
- Next row: P.
- Next row: (K1, m1) twice, K3, (m1, K1) twice. [11 sts]
- Next row: P.
- Next row: K1, (P1, K1) to end.
- Next row: P1, (K1, P1) to end.
- Next row: P1, (K1, P1) to end.
- Next row: K1, (P1, K1) to end.
- Next row: inc1, (P1, K1) to last 2 sts, P1, inc1. [13 sts]
- Next row: P2, (K1, P1) to last st, P1.
- Next row: P2, (K1, P1) to last st, P1.
- Next row: K2, (P1, K1) to last 3 sts, P1, K2.
- Next row: K2, (P1, K1) to last 3 sts, P1, K2.
- Next row: P2, (K1, P1) to last st, P1.
- Next row: P2, (K1, P1) to last st, P1.
- Next row: K2, (P1, K1) to last 3 sts, P1, K2.
- For only the He Crocodile, rep last 4 rows once.

- Next row: k2tog, (P1, K1) to last 3 sts, P1, ssk. [11 sts]
- Next row: P1, (K1, P1) to end.
- Next row: k2tog, P1, (K1, P1) to last 2 sts, ssk. [9 sts]
- Next row: (P1, K1) to last st, P1.
- Next row: (P1, K1) to last st, P1.
- Next row: (K1, P1) to last st, K1.
- Next row: (K1, P1) to last st, K1.
- Next row: (P1, K1) to last st, P1.
- Next row: k2tog, (P1, K1) to last 3 sts, P1, ssk. [7 sts]
- Next row: (P1, K1) to last st, P1.
- Next row: (P1, K1) to last st, P1.
- Next row: (K1, P1) to last st, K1.
- Next row: (K1, P1) to last st, K1.
- Rep last 4 rows once.
- Next row: (P1, K1) to last st, P1.
- Next row: k2tog, P1, K1, P1, ssk. [5 sts]
- Next row: (P1, K1) twice, P1.
- Next row: (P1, K1) twice, P1.
- Next row: (K1, P1) twice, K1.
- Next row: (K1, P1) twice, K1.

- Next row: (P1, K1) twice, P1.
- Next row: k2tog, P1, ssk. [3 sts]
- Next row: P1, K1, P1.
- Next row: P1, K1, P1.
- Next row: K1, P1, K1.
- Next row: s1, k2tog, psso.
- Break yarn and pull it through rem st.

UNDERSIDE
Make 1
- Cast on 7 sts in gray-green.
- 1st row: K1, k2tog, K1, ssk, K1. [5 sts]
- Next row: P.
- Next row: inc1, K2, inc1, K1. [7 sts]
- For the She Crocodile, work 3 rows in St st, beg with a P row.
- For the He Crocodile, work 5 rows in St st, beg with a P row.
- Next row: inc1, K to last 2 sts, inc1, K1. [9 sts]
- Next row: P.
- Rep last 2 rows once more. [11 sts]
- Work 6 rows in St st, beg with a K row.
- Next row: K1, (k2tog) twice, K1, (ssk) twice, K1. [7 sts]
- Next row: P.
- Next row: (K1, m1) twice, K3, (m1, K1) twice. [11 sts]
- Work 5 rows in St st, beg with a P row.
- Next row: K1, m1, K9, m1, K1. [13 sts]
- For the She Crocodile, work 7 rows in St st, beg with a P row.
- For the He Crocodile, work 11 rows in St st, beg with a P row.
- Next row: K1, k2tog, K to last 3 sts, ssk, K1. [11 sts]
- Next row: P.
- Rep last 2 rows once. [9 sts]
- Work 4 rows in St st, beg with a K row.
- Next row: K1, k2tog, K3, ssk, K1. [7 sts]
- Work 9 rows in St st, beg with a P row.
- Next row: K1, k2tog, K1, ssk, K1. [5 sts]

- Work 5 rows in St st, beg with a P row.
- Next row: k2tog, K1, ssk. [3 sts]
- Work 3 rows in St st, beg with a P row.
- Next row: s1, k2tog, psso.
- Break yarn and pull it through rem st.

LEGS
Make 4
- Cast on 7 sts in bottle green.
- K 2 rows.
- Work 6 rows in St st.
- Bind off.

MAKING UP
With the upper body and underside right sides together, whipstitch around the outside, leaving one side of the face open for turning and stuffing. Turn the crocodile right side out and stuff it, shaping it as you go. Sew the gap closed.

Sew the bottom and side seams of the legs using mattress stitch. Stuff the legs lightly. Whipstitch the legs in place on the side of the body so that the tops of the legs overlap the upper body by just under 3⁄8 inch (1 cm) and the seams are on the inside.

Using black yarn, work two French knots for the eyes. Divide a strand of white yarn into two lengthwise and use one of these to work a circle of small chain stitches around each French knot. Using gray-green yarn, work a larger circle of chain stitches around the white chain stitches. For the She Crocodile, using a single strand of black yarn, work a few straight stitches above each eye for the eyelashes.

For the mouth, divide a strand of cream yarn into two lengthwise and use one of these to work a line of chain stitches for the mouth, curving it slightly around the bottom of the eyes.

The Rains Fall

Once the rain had begun, it fell heavily. Dark purplish gray clouds blocked out the sun, and torrents of water poured down from the skies, as if the windows of Heaven had opened. It rained and it rained, and outside the Ark, rivers burst their banks, and the land began to flood. Fields, roads, and villages disappeared as the water got deeper. The Ark lifted off the ground and started to float, while the houses outside were swallowed up by rising floodwater and their occupants drowned.

Looking out of a window, Noah saw the tops of trees vanishing beneath the surface of the water. Soon, even the summits of the mountains had disappeared and there were no remaining signs of life. As God had decreed, all the fowl and cattle and beasts upon the earth had died, along with every man and every creeping insect. Those lucky enough to be on the Ark were the only animals left on the planet, apart from the fish and other creatures that lived in the ocean.

It wasn't very comfortable on the Ark. With so many animals living close together, it soon began to stink. There wasn't much light, but God gave them some precious stones that glowed so they could see their way around, and He made sure that their food stayed fresh.

Noah counted the days—ten, twenty, thirty—and he prayed that God would keep His word and make the rains stop after forty days, because it was very hard being cooped up in the Ark. Everyone longed for the day when they would see dry land again.

Giraffes

Giraffes are the tallest mammals on the earth. Their loftiness means they can graze plants that other animals can't reach and they can keep a good lookout for predators. No two giraffe coats are the same—but for the sake of simplicity, the coats of this couple are both a simple checkered pattern.

You will need

FOR BOTH GIRAFFES

1¾ oz./48 g (131 yd./120 m) of ocher DK yarn

⅛ oz./4 g (11 yd./10 m) of brown DK yarn

Very small amounts of black and white DK yarn

1¾ oz./50 g of polyester toy filling

Use size 2/3 (3 mm) knitting needles, except when instructed to use size 2 (2.75 mm) knitting needles, and a size D-3 (3.25 mm) crochet hook

SHE GIRAFFE
BODY, NECK, AND HEAD

The body, neck, and head are knitted as one piece. The body is knitted first, and the neck and head are knitted onto it.

Make 1

- Cast on 18 sts in ocher and work in ocher except where specified.
- Work 4 rows in St st, beg with a K row.
- Next row: (K2 ocher, K2 brown) 4 times, K2 ocher.
- Next row: (P2 ocher, P2 brown) 4 times, P2 ocher.
- Work 2 rows in St st, beg with a K row.
- Rep last 4 rows 8 times, and break brown yarn.
- Work 4 rows in St st, beg with a K row.
- Bind off.

- Fold the knitted piece in half widthwise and mark the midway point with a thread or small safety pin at the edge of your work.
- With rs facing you, pick up and knit 20 sts from one lower edge of the piece just knitted to the midway marker. With ws facing you, cast on 60 sts. [80 sts]
- Next row: p2tog, P to last 2 sts, p2tog. [78 sts]
- Next row: K2, k2tog, K8, join brown yarn and (K2 brown, K2 ocher) 4 times, K2 brown and break brown yarn leaving a 7½-foot (2-meter) tail, then K18 ocher. Rejoin brown yarn, (K2 brown, K2 ocher) 4 times, K2 brown, then in ocher K8, ssk, K2. [76 sts]
- Next row: p2tog, P9, (P2 brown, P2 ocher) 4 times, P2 brown, P18 ocher, (P2 brown, P2 ocher) 4 times, P2 brown, then in ocher P9, p2tog. [74 sts]
- Next row: K2, k2tog, K to last 4 sts, ssk, K2. [72 sts]
- Next row: p2tog, P to last 2 sts, p2tog. [70 sts]
- Next row: K2, k2tog, K4, (K2 brown, K2 ocher) 4 times, K2 brown, K18 ocher, (K2 brown, K2 ocher) 4 times, K2 brown, then in ocher K4, ssk, K2. [68 sts]
- Next row: p2tog, P5, (P2 brown, P2 ocher) 4 times, P2 brown, P18, (P2 brown, P2 ocher) 4 times, P2 brown, then in ocher P5, p2tog. [66 sts]
- Next row: K2, k2tog, K to last 4 sts, ssk, K2. [64 sts]
- Next row: p2tog, P to last 2 sts, p2tog. [62 sts]
- Next row: Bind off 22 sts, K to end. [40 sts]
- Next row: Bind off 21 sts pwise, P to end. [19 sts]
- Work 3 rows in St st, beg with a K row.
- Next row: k2tog, K to last 2 sts, ssk. [17 sts]
- Next row: K1, k2tog, K to last 3 sts, ssk, K1. [15 sts]
- Next row: P.
- Rep last 2 rows once. [13 sts]
- Next row: K2, (s1, k2tog, psso) 3 times, K2. [7 sts]
- Next row: s1pwise, p2tog, psso, P1, s1pwise, p2tog, psso. [3 sts]
- Break yarn leaving a long yarn tail. Thread the yarn tail through rem sts, pull up the yarn tail, and secure.

FRONT LEGS

Make 2

- Cast on 8 sts in ocher.
- K 4 rows.
- Work 12 rows in St st, beg with a K row.
- Next row: K1, m1, K6, m1, K1. [10 sts]
- Work 9 rows in St st, beg with a P row.
- Bind off.

BACK LEGS

Make 2

- Cast on 8 sts in ocher.
- K 4 rows.
- Work 14 rows in St st, beg with a K row.
- Next row: K1, m1, K6, m1, K1. [10 sts]
- Work 5 rows in St st, beg with a P row.
- Next row: K1, m1, K8, m1, K1. [12 sts]
- Work 9 rows in St st, beg with a P row.
- Bind off.

MANE

Make 1

- Crochet a 9¾-inch (25-cm) chain in brown.

EARS

Make 2

- Using size 2 (2.75 mm) needles, cast on 5 sts in ocher.
- 1st row: inc1, K2, inc1, K1. [7 sts]
- K 7 rows.
- Next row: K1, k2tog, K1, ssk, K1. [5 sts]
- Next row: K.
- Next row: k2tog, K1, ssk. [3 sts]
- Next row: K.
- Next row: s1, k2tog, psso. [1 st]
- Break yarn and pull it through rem st.

HORNS

Make 2

- Using size 2 (2.75 mm) needles, cast on 3 sts in ocher.
- K 3 rows.
- Break ocher yarn and join brown yarn.
- K 3 rows.
- Next row: (K1, m1) twice, K1. [5 sts]
- K 3 rows.
- Next row: k2tog, K1, k2tog. [3 sts]
- Bind off.

TAIL

Make 1

- Cast on 10 sts in ocher.
- K 1 row.
- Bind off.

HE GIRAFFE

BODY, NECK, AND HEAD

The body, neck, and head are knitted as one piece. The body is knitted first, and the neck and head are knitted onto it.

Make 1

- Cast on 18 sts in ocher and work in ocher except where specified.
- Work 6 rows in St st, beg with a K row.
- Next row: (K2 ocher, K2 brown) 4 times, K2 ocher.
- Next row: (P2 ocher, P2 brown) 4 times, P2 ocher.
- Work 2 rows in St st, beg with a K row.
- Rep last 4 rows 9 times. Break brown yarn.
- Work 6 rows in St st, beg with a K row.
- Bind off.

- Fold the knitted piece in half widthwise and mark the midway point with a thread or small safety pin at the edge of your work.
- With rs facing you, pick up and knit 25 sts from one lower edge of the piece just knitted to the midway marker. With ws facing you, cast on 61 sts. [86 sts]
- Next row: p2tog, P to last 2 sts, p2tog. [84 sts]
- Next row: K2, k2tog, K11, join brown yarn and (K2 brown, K2 ocher) 4 times, K2 brown and break brown yarn leaving a 79-inch (2 meter) tail, then K18 ocher, rejoin brown yarn and (K2 brown, K2 ocher) 4 times, K2 brown, then in ocher K11, ssk, K2. [82 sts]
- Next row: p2tog, P12, (P2 brown, P2 ocher) 4 times, P2 brown, P18 ocher, (P2 brown, P2 ocher) 4 times, P2 brown, then in ocher P12, p2tog. [80 sts]
- Next row: K2, k2tog, K to last 4 sts, ssk, K2. [78 sts]
- Next row: p2tog, P to last 2 sts, p2tog. [76 sts]
- Next row: K2, k2tog, K7, (K2 brown, K2 ocher) 4 times, K2 brown, K18 ocher, (K2 brown, K2 ocher) 4 times, K2 brown, then in ocher K7, ssk, K2. [74 sts]
- Next row: p2tog, P8, (P2 brown, P2 ocher) 4 times, P2 brown, P18, (P2 brown, P2 ocher) 4 times, P2 brown, then in ocher P8, p2tog. [72 sts]
- Next row: K2, k2tog, K to last 4 sts, ssk, K2. [70 sts]
- Next row: p2tog, P to last 2 sts, p2tog. [68 sts]

- **Next row:** Bind off 25 sts, K to end. [43 sts]
- **Next row:** Bind off 24 sts pwise, P to end. [19 sts]
- Work 3 rows in St st, beg with a K row.
- **Next row:** k2tog, K to last 2 sts, ssk. [17 sts]
- **Next row:** K1, k2tog, K to last 3 sts, ssk, K1. [15 sts]
- **Next row:** P.
- Rep last 2 rows once. [13 sts]
- **Next row:** K2, (s1, k2tog, psso) 3 times, K2. [7 sts]
- **Next row:** s1pwise, p2tog, psso, P1, s1pwise, p2tog, psso. [3 sts]
- Break yarn leaving a long yarn tail and thread the yarn tail through rem sts. Pull up the yarn tail and secure.

FRONT LEGS
Make 2
- Cast on 8 sts in ocher.
- K 4 rows.
- Work 14 rows in St st, beg with a K row.
- **Next row:** K1, m1, K6, m1, K1. [10 sts]
- Work 11 rows in St st, beg with a P row.
- Bind off.

BACK LEGS
Make 2
- Cast on 8 sts in ocher.
- K 4 rows.
- Work 14 rows in St st, beg with a K row.
- **Next row:** K1, m1, K6, m1, K1. [10 sts]
- Work 7 rows in St st, beg with a P row.
- **Next row:** K1, m1, K8, m1, K1. [12 sts]
- Work 11 rows in St st, beg with a P row.
- Bind off.

MANE
Work as for the She Giraffe.

EARS
Work as for the She Giraffe.

HORNS
Work as for the She Giraffe.

TAIL
Make 1
- Cast on 12 sts in ocher.
- K 1 row.
- Bind off.

MAKING UP
With the right sides of the body, neck, and head piece together, using the yarn tail at the end of the nose, whipstitch the seam at the lower part of the face. Turn the piece the right way out and seam the front of the neck using mattress stitch. Seam the unattached side of the front of the body to the lower part of the neck using mattress stitch. Seam the underside and the back of the neck, again using mattress stitch. Leave the back end open for stuffing. Stuff, then close the gap using mattress stitch.

Seam the lower and side edges of the legs and sew them in place on the sides of the body. The seams should be at the backs of the front legs and on the insides of the back legs.

Pinch the lower edge of the ears together and whipstitch them in place.

Fold the horn pieces in half lengthwise, with the right side on the outside, and whipstitch the two side edges, using matching yarns. Sew the horns in place.

Thread the yarn tail of the mane in and out of the chain through the entire length and gather slightly so that the mane is the same length as the back of the neck. Sew the mane in position.

Whipstitch the long sides of the tail together in the way the piece naturally curls. Add a few loops of the brown yarn to the end of the tail and, if you like, separate the fibers of the yarn, then dampen and rub them together to give the tail a slightly ragged look.

Using black yarn, work two French knots for the eyes. Using white yarn, work a circle of chain stitches around each French knot. For the She Giraffe, using a single strand of black yarn, work a few straight stitches above each eye for the eyelashes.

Using brown yarn, work a large straight stitch for the mouth and work two French knots for the nostrils.

Zebras

You would think that zebras' smartly striped black-and-white coats would make them stick out a mile on the African plains, but they actually provide good camouflage. Zebras tend to move around in big groups, and predators such as lions can't work out the position of individual animals among all the stripes. These knitted versions look a little complicated, but once you get into the swing of knitting stripes, you'll find it easy.

You will need

FOR BOTH ZEBRAS

½ oz./14 g (37 yd./34 m) of white DK yarn

½ oz./14 g (37 yd./34 m) of black DK yarn

Very small amounts of beige and
pale pink DK yarn

1 oz./30 g of polyester toy filling

Use size 2/3 (3 mm) knitting needles, except
when instructed to use size 2 (2.75 mm)
knitting needles

SHE AND HE ZEBRAS

Both zebras are knitted in the same way.

HEAD AND NECK

The head piece is knitted first, and the neck is then knitted onto it.

Make 1

- Cast on 14 sts in white.
- Work 14 rows in a 2 rows white/2 rows black St st pattern, ending with 2 rows worked in white. Break white yarn.
- K 2 rows in black.
- Work 2 rows in St st, beg with a K row.
- Next row: K1, (s1, k2tog, psso) twice, (ssk, transfer last st to left-hand needle, lift the st to the left over transferred st, slip st back to right-hand needle) twice, K1. [6 sts]
- Next row: s1pwise, p2tog, psso, p2tog, transfer last st to left-hand needle, lift the st to the left over transferred st, slip st back to right-hand needle.
- Next row: k2tog, break yarn, and pull it through rem st.

- With rs facing you and nose section pointing to the left, using black yarn, pick up and K 8 sts from the top cast-on edge to the end of the second black stripe. Now pick up and K another 8 sts from the end of the second black stripe on the opposite side, down to the cast-on edge (you will have to twist your work slightly to do this). [16 sts]
- Next row: P.
- Leave black yarn at side and join white yarn.
- Work 6 rows in St st, keeping to the 2 rows white/ 2 rows black pattern, ending with 2 rows worked in white.
- Mark beg and end of last row with a thread or small safety pin.
- Work another 6 rows in St st, keeping to the 2 rows white/2 rows black pattern, ending with 2 rows worked in black.

- Next row: Using white yarn, K8, turn work, and leave rem sts on a stitch holder.
- Next row: Working only on sts just knitted, p2tog, P to end. [7 sts]
- Leave white yarn by side and use black yarn.
- Next row: K to last 2 sts, k2tog. [6 sts]
- Next row: P.
- Keeping to the 2 rows white/2 rows black pattern, rep last 2 rows 4 times. [2 sts]
- Next row: Continuing in black yarn, k2tog. [1 st]
- Break yarns and pull black yarn through rem st.

- With rs of your work facing you, rejoin white yarn to inner edge of lower neck.
- Next row: K. [8 sts]
- Next row: P to last 2 sts, p2tog. [7 sts]
- Leave white yarn by side and join black yarn.
- Next row: k2tog, K to end. [6 sts]
- Next row: P.
- Keeping to the 2 rows white/2 rows black pattern, rep last 2 rows 4 times. [2 sts]
- Next row: Continuing in black yarn, k2tog. [1 st]
- Break yarns and pull black yarn through rem st.

BODY

The body is knitted from the neck edge to the back end.

Make 1

- Cast on 28 sts in white.
- Work 2 rows in St st, beg with a K row.
- Leave white yarn at side and join black yarn.
- Work 16 rows in St st, keeping to the 2 rows black/2 rows white pattern, ending with 2 white rows.
- Bind off tightly.

LEGS

The legs are worked from the foot to the top of the leg.

Make 4

- Cast on 8 sts in black.

- K 4 rows.
- Leave black yarn at side and join white yarn.
- Work 16 rows in St st, keeping to the 2 rows white/2 rows black pattern, ending with 2 black rows.
- Bind off.

EARS
Make 2
- Using size 2 (2.75 mm) needles, cast on 4 sts in white.
- K 5 rows.
- Next row: k2tog, ssk. [2 sts]
- Next row: k2tog.
- Break yarn and pull it through rem st.

MANE
Make 1
- Cast on 16 sts in black.
- 1st row: (K1, P1) to end.
- Bind off, keeping to the K1, P1 pattern.

TAIL
Make 1
- Cast on 8 sts in white.
- Bind off.

MAKING UP
With the right sides of the neck piece together, whipstitch the small seam at the base of the neck.

Fold the body piece in half widthwise and mark the center point of the cast-on edge with a small safety pin or thread. Using mattress stitch, sew one side of the cast-on edge to one side of the neck edge, up to the marker. Sew the other half of the cast-on edge to the other side of the neck edge.

Sew the lower seam of the body using mattress stitch, leaving the back end open for stuffing. Sew the seams at the back of the neck and at the chin using mattress stitch. Stuff fairly lightly to avoid overstretching the stripes. Close the back seam.

Seam the legs using mattress stitch. Stuff the legs and whipstitch them in place. The seams should run up the insides of the legs.

Fold the ear pieces in half lengthwise and whipstitch them in position. Whipstitch the mane in position.

Using black yarn, work two French knots for the eyes. Using beige yarn, work a circle of chain stitches around each French knot. Using white yarn, work a circle of chain stitches around each beige circle.

Using pale pink yarn, work two French knots for the nostrils and a straight stitch for the mouth.

Attach the tail using the yarn tails. For the switch, thread a few short lengths of black yarn through the end of the tail. Knot together tightly and separate some of the strands using the tip of a needle to give a slightly ragged look.

Polar Bears

Polar bears are the world's biggest bears and are right at the top of the Arctic food chain. With their thick fur coats and body fat, they are perfectly adapted to surviving freezing weather. This polar pair has been knitted in a fuzzy white yarn to give the two an extra cuddly look, but you could just as easily knit them in standard white DK yarn.

You will need

FOR BOTH BEARS

1½ oz./42 g (115 yd./105 m) of fluffy white DK yarn

A very small amount of black DK yarn

1¾ oz./50 g of polyester toy filling

Use size 2/3 (3 mm) knitting needles, except when instructed to use size 2 (2.75 mm) knitting needles

SHE BEAR

BODY AND HEAD

The body and head are knitted as one piece from the rear end to the tip of the nose.

Make 1

- Cast on 36 sts in white.
- Work 24 rows in St st, beg with a K row.
- Next row: K9, (k2tog) 3 times, K6, (ssk) 3 times, K9. [30 sts]
- Work 13 rows in St st, beg with a P row.
- Next row: Bind off 5 sts, K6 (7 sts on needle incl st from binding off), (K1, m1) 5 times, K to end. [30 sts]
- Next row: Bind off 5 sts pwise, P to end. [25 sts]
- Next row: K2, (k2tog) twice, K to last 6 sts, (ssk) twice, K2. [21 sts]
- Next row: P.
- Rep last 2 rows once. [17 sts]
- Work 6 rows in St st, beg with a K row.
- Next row: K2, (k2tog) 3 times, K1, (ssk) 3 times, K2. [11 sts]
- Next row: P.
- Next row: K1, (k2tog) twice, K1, (ssk) twice, K1. [7 sts]
- Break yarn and thread it through rem sts. Pull up the yarn tail and secure.

FRONT LEGS

Make 2

- Cast on 13 sts in white.
- K 4 rows.
- Work 16 rows in St st, beg with a K row.
- Bind off.

BACK LEGS

Make 2

- Cast on 13 sts in white.
- K 4 rows.
- Work 20 rows in St st, beg with a K row.
- Bind off.

EARS

Make 2

- Cast on 3 sts in white.
- 1st row: P.
- Next row: (K1, m1) twice, K1. [5 sts]
- Next and every ws row: P.
- Next rs row: k2tog, K1, ssk. [3 sts]
- Next rs row: (K1, m1) twice, K1. [5 sts]
- Next rs row: k2tog, K1, ssk. [3 sts]
- Next row: P.
- Bind off.

TAIL

Make 1

- Cast on 9 sts.
- K 1 row.
- Bind off.

HE BEAR
BODY AND HEAD
The body and head are knitted as one piece from the rear end to the tip of the nose.
Make 1
- Cast on 40 sts in white.
- Work 26 rows in St st, beg with a K row.
- Next row: K10, (k2tog) 3 times, K8, (ssk) 3 times, K10. [34 sts]
- Work 15 rows in St st, beg with a P row.
- Next row: Bind off 6 sts, K8 (9 sts on needle incl st from casting off), (K1, m1) 5 times, K to end. [33 sts]
- Next row: Bind off 6 sts pwise, P to end. [27 sts]
- Next row: K2, (k2tog) twice, K to last 6 sts, (ssk) twice, K2. [23 sts]
- Next row: P.
- Rep last 2 rows once. [19 sts]
- Work 6 rows in St st, beg with a K row.
- Next row: K2, (k2tog) 3 times, K3, (ssk) 3 times, K2. [13 sts]
- Next row: P.
- Next row: K1, (k2tog) twice, K3, (ssk) twice, K1. [9 sts]
- Break yarn and thread it through rem sts. Pull up the yarn tail and secure.

FRONT LEGS
Make 2
- Cast on 14 sts in white.
- K 4 rows.
- Work 18 rows in St st, beg with a K row.
- Bind off.

BACK LEGS
Make 2
- Cast on 14 sts in white.
- K 4 rows.
- Work 22 rows in St st, beg with a K row.
- Bind off.

EARS
Work as for the She Bear.

TAIL
Make 1
- Cast on 10 sts.
- K 1 row.
- Bind off.

MAKING UP
Using the yarn tail at the nose, join the lower seam of the head and body using mattress stitch. Leave the back end open for stuffing. Stuff the body fairly firmly and close the gap using mattress stitch.

Seam the legs using mattress stitch. Stuff the legs and whiptstitch them in place. The seams should run up the insides of the legs.

Fold the ear pieces so that the right side is on the inside. Whipstitch around the curved edges. Turn the ears right side out. Pinch the lower edges of the ears together and sew them in place.

Whipstitch the long sides of the tail together in the way the piece naturally curls. Sew the tail in position.

Using black yarn, work two French knots for the eyes. Using white yarn, work a circle of chain stitches around each French knot. For the She Bear, using a single strand of black yarn, work a few straight stitches above each eye for the eyelashes.

Using black yarn, work the nose in satin stitch and the mouth in straight stitch.

The Ark Comes to Rest on Mount Ararat

On the morning of the forty-first day, Noah woke up and looked out of the window of the Ark. The skies were still dark, but drops of rain were no longer falling. A wind blew gently across the surface of the water, creating ripples.

Noah's family crowded around the window, full of joy that the torrential downpour had finally stopped.

"When do you think we will be able to leave the Ark?" Ham asked hopefully.

But Noah looked out gloomily. No matter which direction he turned, there was no land to be seen. It would take some time before the earth could soak up all that floodwater and the sun could dry the ground. God hadn't mentioned how long they would have to remain onboard. Still, at least it wasn't raining any longer, so they knew it wasn't getting any worse.

More days passed—fifty, sixty, seventy, eighty—and the Ark floated around, carried on the wind and the currents, but nowhere could they see any signs of land. It was seven months and seventeen days after the rain had started when they felt a peculiar sensation one day: a massive jolt that gave them all a fright.

"We've hit something!" Shem cried. "Whatever can it be?"

"The Ark isn't floating anymore," Japheth cried. "That means we must have struck dry land."

They didn't know it at the time, but they had landed on the peak of Mount Ararat, a mountain in the Holy Land. Although they still couldn't see anything but water all around, if the mountaintops were sticking out once more it could only mean one thing: the floodwaters were subsiding.

Penguins

Whether they're tobogganing on their big white tummies or gliding through the water for fish, penguins are one of the most popular creatures around. Perhaps it's their endearing waddle or their stylish black-and-white plumage. Knit a regular penguin or make a little rockhopper penguin by adding some crazy head feathers.

SHE AND HE PENGUINS

Both penguins are knitted in the same way.

BODY AND HEAD
Make 1

- Cast on 12 sts in black.
- Work 18 rows in St st, beg with a K row.
- Next row: K2, k2tog, K4, ssk, K2. [10 sts]
- Next row: P.
- Next row: K1, k2tog, K4, ssk, K1. [8 sts]
- Work 5 rows in St st, beg with a P row.
- Next row: k2tog, K4, ssk. [6 sts]
- Next row: p2tog, P2, p2tog. [4 sts]
- Bind off.

BELLY

Make 1

- Cast on 8 sts in white.
- Work 14 rows in St st, beg with a K row.
- Next row: k2tog, K4, ssk. [6 sts]
- Bind off pwise.

FEET

The feet are knitted from one side to the other.

Make 2

- Using size 1 (2.25 mm) needles, cast on 5 sts in orange.
- 1st row: Bind off 2 sts, K to end. [3 sts]
- Next row: K1, (inc1) twice. [5 sts]
- Rep last 2 rows once. [5 sts]
- Bind off.

BEAK

Make 1

- Divide a piece of orange DK yarn lengthwise into two thinner strands. Using size 1 (2.25 mm) needles, cast on 6 sts with one of the orange strands.
- 1st row: P.
- Next row: k2tog, K2, ssk. [4 sts]
- Next row: (p2tog) twice. [2 sts]
- Next row: k2tog.
- Break yarn and pull it through rem st.

WINGS

Make 2

- Cast on 8 sts in black.
- Work 2 rows in St st, beg with a K row.
- Next row: K1, k2tog, K2, ssk, K1. [6 sts]
- Next row: P.
- Next row: K1, k2tog, ssk, K1. [4 sts]
- Next row: P.
- Next row: k2tog, ssk. [2 sts]
- Next row: p2tog.
- Break yarn and pull it through rem st.

MAKING UP

With the right sides of the body and head pieces together, whipstitch around the head section. Turn right side out and sew the sides using mattress stitch, leaving the bottom open for stuffing. Stuff the penguin and sew the lower edges closed.

Whipstitch the belly patch in place, making sure that the piece is slightly stretched lengthwise before you sew to ensure it lies flat and even.

Fold the wing pieces in half lengthwise, with the right sides facing outward. Whipstitch the edges. Stitch the wings in place on the penguin's sides.

On the feet, thread one of the yarn tails to the opposite side in order to gather the heel end of the foot slightly. Whipstitch the feet in place.

Using black yarn, work two French knots for the eyes. Divide a short length of white yarn into two thinner strands. Use these to work a circle of chain stitches around each French knot.

Fold the beak in half with the right side facing outward and whipstitch the seam. Whipstitch the beak in place on the penguin's face, with the seam on the lower side.

If you like, thread a couple of short pieces of black and yellow yarn through the head and fray them.

Rabbits

These fluffy-tailed beasts can wiggle their tails to communicate with friends and family or thump their hind legs on the ground. Rabbits come in an amazing array of colors—bunny experts estimate there are more than 150 combinations—so you can pretty much choose whatever color you like. While their real-life relatives are known for their reproductive powers, if you want to have more of this particular rabbit breed, you will have to get knitting.

You will need

FOR BOTH RABBITS

¼ oz./8 g (20 yd./18 m) of caramel DK yarn

⅛ oz./4 g (11 yd./10 m) of black DK yarn

⅛ oz./4 g (9 yd./8 m) of white DK yarn

Small amounts of white mohair yarn and beige DK yarn

⅜ oz./10 g of polyester toy filling

Use size 2/3 (3 mm) knitting needles, except when instructed to use size 2 (2.75 mm) knitting needles

SHE AND HE RABBITS

Both rabbits are knitted with the same pattern. The main instructions are for the She Rabbit (caramel). The colors and any different instructions for the He Rabbit (black and white) are given in parentheses within the instructions.

BODY

The body is knitted from the neck edge to the rear end.
Make 1

- Cast on 18 sts in caramel (black).
- Work 16 rows in St st, beg with a K row. (Work 6 rows in St st in black, 4 rows in white mohair, and 6 rows in black, beg with a K row.)
- Next row: Continuing in caramel (black), K2, k2tog, K10, ssk, K2. [16 sts]
- Next row: p2tog, P12, p2tog. [14 sts]
- Bind off.

HEAD

The head pieces are knitted from the top to the lower edge.
FRONT
Make 1

- Cast on 5 sts in caramel (white).
- Work 2 rows in St st, beg with a K row.
- Next row: (K1, m1) twice, K1, (m1, K1) twice. [9 sts]
- Next and every ws row unless stated otherwise: P.
- Next rs row: K1, m1, K7, m1, K1. [11 sts]
- Next rs row: K.

- **Next rs row:** K5, m1, K1, m1, turn work and P3, turn work again, and K to end. [13 sts]
- **Next rs row:** K5, s1, k2tog, psso, K5. [11 sts]
- **Next row:** p2tog, P7, p2tog. [9 sts]
- **Next row:** K1, k2tog, K3, ssk, K1. [7 sts]
- **Next row:** P.
- **Bind off.**

BACK
Make 1
- **Cast on 5 sts in caramel (white).**
- **Work 2 rows in St st, beg with a K row.**
- **Next row:** (K1, m1) twice, K1, (m1, K1) twice. [9 sts]
- **Next row:** P.
- **Next row:** K1, m1, K7, m1, K1. [11 sts]
- **Work 6 rows in St st, beg with a P row.**
- **Next row:** p2tog, P7, p2tog. [9 sts]
- **Next row:** K1, k2tog, K3, ssk, K1. [7 sts]
- **Next row:** P.
- **Bind off.**

FRONT LEGS
Make 2
- **Cast on 7 sts in caramel (white).**
- **Work 10 rows in St st, beg with a K row.**
- **Bind off.**

BACK LEGS
The back legs are knitted from the sole of the foot upward.
Make 2
- **Cast on 15 sts in caramel (black).**
- **Work 2 rows in St st, beg with a K row.**
- **Next row:** Bind off 4 sts, K to end. [11 sts]
- **Next row:** Bind off 4 sts pwise, P to end. [7 sts]
- **Work 2 rows in St st, beg with a K row.**
- **Next row:** K2, m1, K to last 2 sts, m1, K2. [9 sts]
- **Next row:** P.
- **Rep last 2 rows once.** [11 sts]
- **Next row:** K2, m1, K7, m1, K2. [13 sts]
- **Next row:** p2tog, P9, p2tog. [11 sts]
- **Bind off.**

EARS
Make 2
- **Cast on 3 sts in caramel (black).**
- **K 14 rows.**
- **Next row:** s1, k2tog, psso.
- **Break yarn and pull it through rem st.**

TAIL
Make 1
- **Using a double strand of white mohair yarn, cast on 5 sts.**
- **K 4 rows.**
- **Bind off.**

MAKING UP
Place the two head pieces right sides together and whipstitch around the edge, leaving a gap at the lower edge. Turn the head right side out through this gap, stuff the head, and close the gap.

Using mattress stitch, join the lower and back seams of the body piece, leaving the neck end open. Stuff the body. Whipstitch the neck edge to the back of the head, so that the neck forms a circle on the back of the head.

Seam the front legs using mattress stitch and whipstitch them in place. The seams should run up the insides of the legs. Fold the back leg pieces right sides together and whipstitch along the lower edges and the front of the feet. Turn right side out. Seam the rest of the leg pieces using mattress stitch, stuffing as you go. Whipstitch the legs in place.

Make a small pleat at the bottom of the ears and sew them in place with a couple of stitches.

Fold the tail piece in half lengthwise and whipstitch the seam. Sew the tail in position.

Using black yarn, work two French knots for the eyes. With white yarn (beige yarn for the black-and-white rabbit), work a circle of chain stitches around each French knot. (For the black-and-white rabbit, work another circle of black chain stitches around one eye.) Use a single strand of black yarn to work three straight stitches in a Y shape for the nose and, for the caramel rabbit, use a second strand to work a few straight stitches above each eye for the eyelashes.

Tortoises

The tortoise is one of the oldest species on the earth, and many tortoises live to be more than 100 years old. Their hard, domed shells keep them safe from would-be predators. The giant tortoises of the Galapagos Islands are probably the most famous in the world—but some species are so small that they would fit into the palm of your hand and are barely bigger than the woolly reptiles shown here.

You will need

FOR BOTH TORTOISES

⅛ oz./3 g (7 yd./6 m) of medium green DK yarn

⅛ oz./3 g (7 yd./6 m) of khaki DK yarn

⅛ oz./4 g (10 yd./9 m) of beige DK yarn

Small amounts of black and medium brown DK yarn

Very small amounts of white and red DK yarn

⅜ oz./10 g of polyester toy filling

Use size 2/3 (3 mm) knitting needles

SHE AND HE TORTOISES

Both tortoises are knitted with the same pattern. The main instructions are for the She Tortoise (green and brown). The colors for the He Tortoise (khaki and black) are given in parentheses within the instructions.

SHELL

The shell is knitted from the bottom end to the head end.

Make 1

- Cast on 6 sts in medium green (khaki).
- 1st row: inc1, K3, inc1, K1. [8 sts]
- Next row: K.
- Next row: K1, m1, K to last st, m1, K1. [10 sts]
- Next row: K2, P to last 2 sts, K2.
- Rep last 2 rows 3 times. [16 sts]
- Next row: K.
- Next row: K2, P to last 2 sts, K2.
- Rep last 2 rows twice.
- Next row: K1, k2tog, K to last 3 sts, ssk, K1. [14 sts]
- Next row: K2, P to last 2 sts, K2.
- Rep last 2 rows twice. [10 sts]
- Next row: K1, k2tog, K4, ssk, K1. [8 sts]
- Next row: k2tog, K4, ssk. [6 sts]
- Bind off.

UNDERSIDE

The underside is knitted from the bottom end to the head end.

Make 1

- Cast on 4 sts in beige.
- 1st row: inc1, K1, inc1, K1. [6 sts]
- Next row: K1, m1, K to last st, m1, K1. [8 sts]
- Next row: P.
- Rep last 2 rows 3 times. [14 sts]
- Work 6 rows in St st, beg with a K row.
- Next row: K1, k2tog, K to last 3 sts, ssk, K1. [12 sts]
- Next row: P.
- Rep last 2 rows twice. [8 sts]
- Next row: K1, k2tog, K2, ssk, K1. [6 sts]
- Bind off pwise.

HEAD

Make 1

- Cast on 13 sts in beige.
- Work 4 rows in St st, beg with a K row.
- Next row: K1, (k2tog) twice, K3, (ssk) twice, K1. [9 sts]
- Next row: (p2tog) twice, P1, (p2tog) twice. [5 sts]
- Break yarn and thread it through rem sts. Pull up tightly and secure.

LEGS

The legs are worked from the top edge that joins the shell to the toes.

Make 4

- Cast on 6 sts in beige.
- Work 4 rows in St st, beg with a K row.
- Next row: k2tog, K2, ssk. [4 sts]
- Break yarn and thread it through rem sts. Pull up tightly and secure.

MAKING UP

Join the shell to the underside of the tortoise by working a running stitch around the edge, about ¼ inch (5 mm) in from the edge, leaving a gap at the neck end for stuffing. Stuff the tortoise body, shaping it into a dome as you go, and close the gap. Using brown (black) yarn, work lines of chain stitches down and across the shell to represent the markings.

Sew the back seam of the head using mattress stitch, leaving the lower edge open for stuffing. Stuff the head lightly and whipstitch the base of it to the front edge of the underside, making sure that the back seam of the head runs down the center back of the head. Work a couple of stitches at the back of the head to secure it on the shell.

Sew the back seams of the legs. The legs do not need stuffing. Secure the top of the legs to the underside of the body, making sure the seams are on the underside.

Using black yarn, work two French knots for the eyes. Using white yarn, work a circle of chain stitches around each French knot. For the She Tortoise, using a single strand of black yarn, work a few straight stitches above each eye for the eyelashes.

Separate a short length of red yarn into two thinner strands and use one of these to work a V shape for the mouth in straight stitches.

The Raven, the Dove, and the Olive Leaf

Every day without fail, his sons asked Noah, "How much longer until we can leave the Ark?"

Noah was a clever man and he came up with a plan to test how much the waters had receded.

First of all, he found a black raven, and he released it from the Ark—but the glossy-feathered bird just circled around and around and didn't want to fly any farther away because it couldn't see anywhere to land. Eventually, Noah let it come back inside to safety.

Next, Noah decided to try releasing a white dove. The dove flew some distance away from the Ark but couldn't find anywhere to land, so she circled around and came back to rest on Noah's outstretched hand.

"We must wait a while longer," Noah said, and they all sighed in unison.

Seven days later, Noah decided to try again. He released the white dove, and she flew away out of sight. He waited and waited, and some hours later, just as evening was falling, the dove returned with a small branch of an olive tree in its beak.

Noah cheered out loud. That meant the waters were now lower than the treetops, and green plants were beginning to grow again. It was a wonderful sight.

After another seven days, Noah released the dove yet again. She flew off, and he waited all day by the window of the Ark, but night fell, and the dove still hadn't returned. This was great news, because it meant that she had found somewhere to nest on dry land. Their troubles were almost over.

Goats

Goats were one of the first animals to be domesticated by humans. They come in a dazzling mix of tones of gray, brown, black, cream, and russet. Gray and brown are the main colors for this pair, and there's a small amount of cream mohair yarn for some extra fuzziness—but you could just as easily use other earthy shades.

SHE AND HE GOATS

Both the She and He Goat are knitted with the same pattern, but the colors are different. The main pattern is for the She Goat (brown), with the colors for the He Goat (gray) given in parentheses within the instructions.

BODY AND HEAD

Make 1

- Cast on 24 sts in brown (medium gray).
- Work 8 rows in St st, beg with a K row.
- Leave brown (medium gray) yarn by side and join cream mohair yarn.
- Work 6 rows in St st, beg with a K row.
- Break yarn and rejoin brown (medium gray) yarn.
- Work 6 rows in St st, beg with a K row.
- Next row: Bind off 12 sts, K to end. [12 sts]
- Next row: P.
- Next row: Cast on 27 sts, K to end. [39 sts]
- Next row: p2tog, P to last 2 sts, p2tog. [37 sts]
- Next row: K1, k2tog, K to last 3 sts, ssk, K1. [35 sts]
- Rep last 2 rows twice. [27 sts]
- Next row: p2tog, P to last 2 sts, p2tog. [25 sts]
- Next row: Bind off 4 sts, K to end. [21 sts]

You will need

FOR BOTH GOATS

¼ oz./8 g (20 yd./18 m) of brown DK yarn

¼ oz./8 g (20 yd./18 m) of medium gray DK yarn

⅛ oz./4 g (11 yd./10 m) of cream mohair yarn

Small amounts of beige, dark cream, dark gray, and pale gray DK yarn

Very small amounts of black and camel DK yarn

¾ oz./20 g of polyester toy filling

Use size 2/3 (3 mm) knitting needles, except when instructed to use size 2 (2.75 mm) knitting needles

- Next row: Bind off 4 sts pwise, P to end. [17 sts]
- Next row: K.
- Next row: P.
- Next row: K1, k2tog, K to last 3 sts, s1, K1, psso, K1. [15 sts]
- Next row: p2tog, P to last 2 sts, p2tog. [13 sts]
- Next row: K1, k2tog, K to last 3 sts, s1, k1, psso, K1. [11 sts]
- Next row: (p2tog) twice, s1pwise, p2tog, psso, (p2tog) twice. [5 sts]
- Break yarn, leaving a long tail. Thread the yarn tail through the rem sts.

BACK LEGS
Make 2
- Cast on 9 sts in cream mohair.
- K 3 rows.
- Work 10 rows in St st, beg with a K row.
- Break yarn and join brown (medium gray) yarn.
- Work 8 rows in St st, beg with a K row.
- Bind off.

FRONT LEGS
Make 2
- Cast on 9 sts in cream mohair.
- K 3 rows.
- Work 8 rows in St st, beg with a K row.
- Break yarn and join brown (medium gray) yarn.
- Work 8 rows in St st, beg with a K row.
- Bind off.

TAIL
Make 1
- Cast on 10 sts in brown (medium gray).
- Bind off.

EARS
Make 2
- Using size 2 (2.75 mm) needles, cast on 4 sts in beige (dark gray).
- K 1 row.

- Next row: K1, m1, K2, m1, K1. [6 sts]
- K 5 rows.
- Next row: K1, (k2tog) twice, K1. [4 sts]
- Next row: K.
- Next row: (k2tog) twice. [2 sts]
- Next row: K.
- Next row: k2tog. [1 st]
- Break yarn and pull it through rem st.

SHE GOAT LONG HORNS
Make 2
- Cast on 11 sts in dark cream.
- Bind off.

HE GOAT SHORT HORNS
Make 2
- Cast on 4 sts in pale gray.
- Bind off.

MAKING UP
Pull the yarn tail at the end of the nose fairly tight and secure. Use the yarn tail to sew together the chin, the front of the neck, and the underside using mattress stitch. Leave the back open for stuffing. Stuff the goat, then close the gap using mattress stitch.

Seam the legs using mattress stitch and whipstitch them in place. The seams should run up the insides of the legs.

Sew the tail in place.

Fold the ears in half lengthwise and whipstitch them in position. Stitch the horns in position.

For the eyes on the He Goat, work a small oval in chain stitch using camel yarn. For the eyes on the She Goat, work a small oval in chain stitch using dark cream yarn. For the pupils, split a short length of black yarn in two lengthwise. Use one of these strands to work two small straight stitches, one over the top of the other, in the center of each eye.

For the mouth and nose of the He Goat, work three straight stitches in a Y shape using black yarn. For the She Goat, do the same using beige yarn.

For the beard on the He Goat, tie a few short lengths of medium gray yarn on the chin and fray them.

Pigs

It's true that pigs like to wallow in a little mud to keep cool, especially if there's no water around, but in the personal-hygiene department, pigs are one of the cleanest animals around. This handsome pair are knitted in the palest of pinks—but you could knit them in gray, black, or brown, if you prefer, and even add a few embroidered spots.

You will need

FOR BOTH PIGS

½ oz./12 g (31 yd./28 m) of
pale pink DK yarn

A small amount of medium gray DK yarn

Very small amounts of black,
white, and dark pink DK yarn

½ oz./15 g of polyester toy filling

Use size 2/3 (3 mm) knitting needles
and a size D-3 (3.25 mm) crochet hook

SHE PIG

BODY AND HEAD
Make 1

- Cast on 22 sts in pale pink.
- 1st row: K4, inc1, K11, inc1, K5. [24 sts]
- Next row: P.
- Next row: K6, m1, K12, m1, K6. [26 sts]
- Work 17 rows in St st, beg with a P row.
- Next row: K3, (k2tog) 4 times, K4, (ssk) 4 times, K3. [18 sts]
- Work 3 rows in St st, beg with a P row.
- Next row: K5, k2tog, K4, s1, K1, psso, K5. [16 sts]
- Next row: P.
- Next row: K5, k2tog, K2, s1, K1, psso, K5. [14 sts]
- Next row: P.
- Next row: K1, k2tog, K2, k2tog, s1, K1, psso, K2, ssk, K1. [10 sts]
- Next row: P.
- Next row: K1, k2tog, K4, s1, K1, psso, K1. [8 sts]
- Next row: K.
- Break yarn, leaving a long yarn tail. Thread it through rem sts and pull up fairly tight.

EARS
Make 2

- Cast on 4 sts in pale pink.
- 1st row: inc1, K1, inc1, K1. [6 sts]
- Next and every ws row: P.
- Next row: k2tog, K2, s1, K1, psso. [4 sts]
- Next rs row: k2tog, s1, K1, psso. [2 sts}
- Next rs row: k2tog.
- Break yarn and pull it through rem st.

LEGS
Make 4

- Cast on 7 sts in pale pink.
- K 2 rows.
- Work 8 rows in St st.
- Bind off.

TAIL
Make 1

Using a doubled length of pale pink yarn, crochet a 1¼-inch (3 cm) chain. Trim the ends to about ⅜ inch (1 cm) and separate the yarn strands for the tail switch.

HE PIG

BODY AND HEAD
Make 1

- Cast on 24 sts in pale pink.
- 1st row: K5, inc1, K12, inc1, K5. [26 sts]
- Next row: P.
- Next row: K7, m1, K12, m1, K7. [28 sts]
- Work 7 rows in St st, beg with a P row.
- Leave pink yarn by side and join medium gray yarn.
- Work 6 rows in St st, beg with a K row.
- Break yarn and rejoin pale pink yarn.
- Work 6 rows in St st, beg with a K row.
- Next row: K4, (k2tog) 4 times, K4, (ssk) 4 times, K4. [20 sts]
- Work 3 rows in St st, beg with a P row.
- Next row: K6, k2tog, K4, s1, K1, psso, K6. [18 sts]
- Next row: P.
- Next row: K6, k2tog, K2, s1, K1, psso, K6. [16 sts]
- Next row: P.
- Next row: (K2, k2tog) twice, s1, K1, psso, K2, ssk, K2. [12 sts]
- Next row: P.
- Next row: K2, k2tog, K4, s1, K1, psso, K2. [10 sts]
- Next row: K.
- Break yarn, leaving a long tail. Thread the yarn tail through the rem sts.

EARS
Work as for the She Pig.

LEGS

Make 4

- **Cast on 7 sts in pale pink.**
- **K 2 rows.**
- **Work 10 rows in St st.**
- **Bind off.**

TAIL

Work as for the She Pig.

MAKING UP

Pull the yarn tail at the end of the nose fairly tight and secure. Use the yarn tail to sew the underside of the head and body using mattress stitch, leaving a gap at the back of the pig for stuffing. Stuff the pig and sew the back seam closed.

Sew the leg seams using mattress stitch. Stuff the legs and whipstitch them in place. The seams should run up the insides of the legs.

Fold the ears in half lengthwise, so that the right side is facing outward, and whipstitch them in place.

Sew the tails in place, curling them and securing the curl with a stitch.

Using black yarn, make two French knots for the eyes. Because pigs' eyes are small, wind your yarn just once around your needle when making the French knots. Separate a length of white yarn lengthwise into two thinner strands. Use one of these to work a circle of small chain stitch around each French knot. For the She Pig, use a single strand of black yarn to work a few straight stitches above each eye for the eyelashes.

Separate a length of dark pink yarn lengthwise into two thinner strands. Use one of these to work two straight stitches, one on top of the other, for the mouth. For the nostrils, make two small straight stitches using a single strand of the same yarn.

Raven and Dove

Ravens are big, cackling birds that are usually seen in noisy groups. This and the fact that they normally feed on dead animals mean that they don't have a great reputation. This woolly raven will help set that reputation right. The white dove has become a symbol of love and peace—probably due in part to the bird's sweet nature, but also because of its role in the story of Noah's Ark. This little woolly dove is small and quick to knit.

You will need

FOR THE RAVEN

⅛ oz./4 g (11yd./10 m) of black DK yarn

Very small amounts of white and dark gray DK yarn

A small amount of polyester toy filling

FOR THE DOVE

1/16 oz./2 g (5½ yd./5 m) of white DK yarn

Very small amounts of black, cream, and brown DK yarn

A very small amount of cream mohair yarn

A small amount of polyester toy filling

Use size 2/3 (3 mm) knitting needles, except when instructed to use size 1 (2.25 mm) knitting needles, and a size D-3 (3.25 mm) crochet hook

RAVEN
HEAD AND BODY
FIRST SIDE
Make 1

- Cast on 6 sts in black.
- 1st row: inc1, K3, inc1, K1. [8 sts]
- Next and every ws row unless stated otherwise: P.
- Next rs row: (K1, m1) twice, K4, (m1, K1) twice. [12 sts]
- Next rs row: K1, m1, K10, m1, k1. [14 sts]
- Next rs row: K1, m1, K12, m1, k1. [16 sts] *
- Next rs row: Cast on 5 sts, K to end. [21 sts]
- Next rs row: Bind off 8 sts, K to end. [13 sts]
- Next rs row: k2tog, K to end. [12 sts]
- Next rs row: Bind off 5 sts, K to end. [7 sts]
- Next rs row: Bind off 1 st, K to end. [6 sts]
- Next rs row: K.
- Next rs row: k2tog, K2, ssk. [4 sts]
- Next row: (p2tog) twice. [2 sts]
- Next row: k2tog.
- Break yarn and pull it through rem st.

SECOND SIDE
Make 1

- Work as for first side to *.
- Next row: Cast on 5 sts pwise, P to end. [21 sts]
- Next and every rs row unless stated otherwise: K.
- Next ws row: Bind off 8 sts pwise, P to end. [13 sts]
- Next ws row: p2tog, P to end. [12 sts]
- Next ws row: Bind off 5 sts pwise, P to end. [7 sts]
- Next ws row: Bind off 1 st pwise, P to end. [6 sts]
- Next ws row: P.
- Next ws row: P.
- Next row: k2tog, K2, ssk. [4 sts]
- Next row: (p2tog) twice. [2 sts]
- Next row: k2tog.
- Break yarn and pull it through rem st.

WINGS
Make 2

- Cast on 4 sts in black.
- Work 8 rows in St st, beg with a K row.
- Next row: k2tog, ssk. [2 sts]
- Next row: p2tog.
- Break yarn and pull it through rem st.

BEAK
Make 1

- Divide a length of dark gray yarn into two thinner strands. Using size 1 (2.25 mm) needles, cast on 6 sts in separated yarn.
- 1st row: P.
- Next row: k2tog, K2, ssk. [4 sts]
- Next row: (p2tog) twice. [2 sts]
- Next row: k2tog.
- Break yarn and pull it through rem st.

MAKING UP
Place the two body pieces right sides together. Whipstitch around the edges, leaving the lower edge of the body open. Turn right side out, stuff the raven, and sew the gap closed.

Whipstitch the front part of the wings to the raven's body, leaving the end parts free.

Using black yarn, embroider two French knots for the eyes. Divide a short length of white yarn into two thinner strands. Use these to work a circle of chain stitch around each French knot.

Fold the beak in half, with the right side facing outward, and whipstitch the seam. Whipstitch the beak in place on the raven's head, with the seam underneath.

DOVE
HEAD AND BODY
FIRST SIDE
Make 1

- Cast on 4 sts in white.
- 1st row: inc1, K1, inc1, K1. [6 sts]
- Next and every ws row unless stated otherwise: P.
- Next rs row: (K1, m1) twice, K2, (m1, K1) twice. [10 sts]
- Next rs row: K1, m1, K8, m1, K1. [12 sts]
- Next rs row: K1, m1, K10, m1, K1. [14 sts]
- Next rs row: K. *
- Next rs row: Bind off 8 sts, K to end. [6 sts]
- Next rs row: s1, K1, psso, K4. [5 sts]
- Next rs row: K.
- Next rs row: s1, K1, psso, K1, ssk. [3 sts]
- Next rs row: s1, k2tog, psso.
- Break yarn and pull it through rem st.

SECOND SIDE
Make 1

- Work as for first side to *.
- Next row: Bind off 8 sts pwise, P to end. [6 sts]
- Next row: K.
- Next and every ws row unless stated otherwise: P.
- Next rs row: K4, ssk. [5 sts]
- Next rs row: K.
- Next rs row: s1, K1, psso, K1, ssk. [3 sts]
- Next rs row: s1, k2tog, psso.
- Break yarn and pull it through rem st.

BEAK
Make 1
Crochet a chain of 2 stitches in brown.

WINGS
FIRST WING
- **Cast on 5 sts in white.**
- **1st row: inc1, K1, ssk, K1. [5 sts]**
- **Next row: P.**
- **Rep last 2 rows once.**
- *** Next row: K.**
- **Next row: p2tog, P1, p2tog. [3 sts]**
- **Next row: K.**
- **Next row: P.**
- **Next row: s1, k2tog, psso.**
- **Break yarn and pull it through rem st.**

SECOND WING
- **Cast on 5 sts in white.**
- **1st row: K1, k2tog, inc1, K1. [5 sts]**
- **Next row: P.**
- **Rep last 2 rows once.**
- **Work as for first wing from *.**

MAKING UP
Place the two body pieces right sides together. Whipstitch around the edges, leaving the lower edge open. Turn right side out, stuff the dove, and sew the gap closed.

Whipstitch the front part of the wings to the dove's body, leaving the end parts free. Arrange a few loops of cream mohair yarn in place for the dove's tail.

Separate a length of black yarn into two thinner strands. Use one of these to work two French knots for the eyes. Because the eyes are small, wind your yarn just once around your needle when making the French knots. Separate a length of white yarn into two thinner strands and use one of these to work a circle of chain stitch around each French knot. Using a single strand of black yarn, work a few small straight stitches above each eye for the eyelashes.

Fold the chain for the beak in half and sew it in place using the yarn tails.

Noah Thanks the Lord

After more than a year onboard, Noah opened the great wooden door of the Ark and rejoiced when he saw that there was dry land outside. The sun shone, and everything looked fresh and clean and new.

God spoke to him: "Go forth," He said, "You and your wife and your sons and your sons' wives. Take with you all the fowl and the cattle, all the beasts and creeping things, and be fruitful and multiply."

Noah lowered the gangplank and let his family and all of the animals walk down onto solid ground again. It felt strange after such a long time afloat. It took awhile to get used to being back on land, but soon the grazing animals wandered off to look for grass and the birds flew away to build nests, while the monkeys headed for the nearest trees. The first thing Noah did was to build an altar to thank God for saving him and his family.

God was so pleased with Noah that He created a beautiful rainbow, which curved through the bright blue skies.

"This is a token of the promise I make to you," He said, "that I will never again send a flood to destroy all flesh."

Noah and his wife and his sons and their wives had a lot of children, and their children had children, who also had children. Today, every human being is a direct descendant of Noah and his family. If it weren't for all his hard work in building the Ark and collecting breeding pairs of every kind of animal, none of us would exist, and the world today would be a very different place.

Index